D1555034

Inside the kingdom of God is a temple.

Inside the temple is a daughter of Zion.

Inside the daughter of Zion is a quiet heart.

Inside the quiet heart is God's sanctuary.

"I will be to them as a little sanctuary . . .

saith the Lord." *(Ezekiel 11:16)*

A Quiet Heart

Patricia T. Holland

BOOKCRAFT

Library of Congress Cataloging-in-Publication Data

Holland, Patricia T., 1942–
    A quiet heart / Patricia T. Holland.
        p.   cm.
    ISBN 1-57345-801-5
    1. Mormon women—Religious life.   2. Spiritual life—Church of Jesus Christ of Latter-day Saints.   I. Title.
    BX8641.H65   2000
    248.4'89332—dc21

                                                    00-040387

Printed in the United States of America   72076-0227R
Publishers Printing, Salt Lake City, UT

10   9

Contents

⟋⟍

For my parents, M. W. and Marilla Terry,

who loved me and gave me faith

Acknowledgments

This book would never have been pursued or published if it had not been for the loving and persistent encouragement of Sheri Dew. Later Emily Watts brought skill and sensitivity to the task of editing. I am grateful for Tom Hewitson's careful and creative design. My thanks also to my friend Shari McLean for her cover photograph of a peace rose.

I especially wish to thank my husband, who has given me what every woman desires—love, strength, encouragement, and belief in my own worth. It was he who introduced me to daily scripture study. It was he who taught me that prayers are answered in a variety of ways but they are always answered. It was his unfailing faith that led me to understand true joy can only come from a rich inner life.

Above all else I wish to thank my Father in heaven for blessings beyond expression. He has given me all that I love and all that I believe. With greater and greater emphasis on simplicity, he has given me all that I need. He will be my Sanctuary forever.

1

"Filled with All the Fulness of God"

"[Christ is] the light of the sun . . . the moon . . . the stars . . . and the earth also, . . . which light proceedeth forth from the presence of God to fill the immensity of space. . . . The day shall come when you shall comprehend even God, being quickened in him and by him. Then shall ye know that ye have seen me, that I am, and that I am the true light that is in you, and that you are in me; otherwise ye could not abound" (D&C 88:7–10, 12, 49–50).

Every human heart desires to "abound" in God. That can come only through the light by which God quickens us. Illuminated hearts become filled with charity—for ourselves, for others, and for God, who perpetuates that cycle until charity fills the emptiness of any space. Therefore the Lord tells us, "Above all things, clothe yourselves with the bond of charity" (D&C 88:125).

We cannot give love or strength that we do not ourselves have. So if we expect to clothe ourselves with the bond of charity—if we hope to bless others with God's truths and compassion and sustenance—then we must spend more time with God in a very direct way. We do not have to rely on anyone else's witness of the Father. We can have direct encounters of our own. As Paul told the Ephesians, we can literally be "filled with all the fulness of God" (Ephesians 3:19). Those encounters can fill and refill our cups every day of our lives.

Paul's promise seems especially relevant because more and more we live in a world that can be frighteningly empty. Those who don't have the gospel, both near home and around the globe, often create ineffective communities, work in stress-filled professions, and have declining morals, ruined health, failing families, and in the end, failing hope.

One especially troubling complaint of our time is there is no commonality among women. Across cultures and countries and even in our own neighborhoods, we women have become so diverse and so separated in our lifestyles, interests, and preoccupations that rarely do we have a friend such as our mothers had over the back fence, a neighbor to visit, to love, and to talk with. But we still need someone to listen when our joints ache, our children squabble, or (perhaps even more urgently) when we wish we had squabbling children or loved ones nearby to nurture. We must not let the modern world isolate, fragment, or distance us from those we can love and serve.

Isolation can be one of the most frightening and stressful

circumstances of the human heart. We all need other people and strong, sweet relationships. The Church helps us with that. Relief Society offers us a sisterhood that we can cherish, an association with others who believe what we believe, who hope what we hope, and who love the things of God.

To receive the fulness God has intended for us, to offset the emptiness of isolation or hurt or sorrow, to clothe ourselves "with the bond of charity, as with a mantle" (D&C 88:125), we are all going to have to reach out with our hearts and let down some barriers. Most of us protect ourselves from pain—hurtful experiences and words that come from our friends, our enemies, and sometimes from within us—by building walls, emotional defenses around our hearts.

But the same walls we build to protect ourselves can also isolate us, and that isolation leads to the problems we see so many others struggling with. Can we let down a few walls and find that we are in the embrace of God? Let's receive the spirit of holiness and let our cups be filled with living water. Let us receive in order to give.

One of my foundation stones for trusting that this can happen is a powerful statement from President George Q. Cannon: "No matter how serious the trial, how deep the distress, how great the affliction, [God] will never desert us. He never has, and He never will. He cannot do it. It is not His character. He is an unchangeable being; the same yesterday, the same today, and He will be the same throughout the eternal ages to come. We have found that God. We have made Him our friend, obeying His gospel; and He will stand by us. We may pass through the fiery furnace; we may pass through deep waters but we shall not be consumed nor overwhelmed. We shall emerge from all these trials and difficulties the better and purer for them, if we only trust in our God and keep His commandments" (*Collected Discourses*, comp. Brian H. Stuy [B. H. S. Publishing, 1988], 2:185).

I would place that theology right at the heart of the gospel. We have every right to be hopeful. We have every right to have faith. God lives and loves us. He will not desert us. We can let down a few of our defenses against a faithless world.

Paul wrote, "*Be not conformed to this world: but be ye transformed by the renewing of your mind, that ye may prove what is that good, and acceptable, and perfect, will of God*" (Romans 12:2; emphasis added). To connect with God and be filled with his fulness, to resist conforming to the world, and to discover "that good, and acceptable, and perfect, will of God" *for us* requires a settled, calm mind, a "renewed mind," as Paul suggests, a spirit of contentment, a divine trust and serenity, and a willingness to surrender to God's will. A renewed mind is one that has been illuminated by a new spiritual perception—revelation. When our minds have been illuminated to see as God sees, it becomes a joy to accept his will.

At a time when my oldest son was still single and wanting so much to be married, I was anxiously pleading with the Lord to bless him. My request was very specific; I knew what my son needed. As I was pleading (with an eye fixed on my needs and my anxieties), asking the Lord to please bless him, the words came resoundingly into my mind, "I *am* blessing him. Be patient with my plan." I was stunned— moved to tears. I realized I had been commanding heaven, saying, "Lord, here is your work as I have outlined it. Please notify me when you have bestowed my blessings, pursued my plans, and carried out my will."

In sweet reply comes the mild rebuke, "If you don't mind, Patricia, I prefer to bestow my blessings and to do it in my way." When we can feel sure that God has not forgotten us—nor will he ever—and that he is blessing us in his own way, then the world seems a better, safer place. If we can be patient with his process—which simply means having faith—if we can commune personally and often with him, we can spare ourselves the emptiness and frenzy we feel if we are "conformed to the world": fainthearted, impatient, troubled by envy or greed or pride of a thousand kinds. We

can keep our minds fixed enough on eternity to remember that God's ways are not our ways (see Isaiah 55:8–9).

Isn't it sometimes discouraging to see just how easily the adversary uses such earthly issues as vanity and worry, envy and pettiness to distract us from our divine mission and the unity we could enjoy in the Church? We all get discouraged and distracted—caught up in the thick of thin things—no matter how good we are. But do we have time, energy, or emotion to waste on what dress to wear or whose living room is the loveliest? We have real things to think about, things of the kingdom of God. We need to drink more deeply and be filled more fully for the work that lies ahead of us.

Let me suggest some ways that this fulness can come. Often when I face difficulties, I need to turn off the phone, lock the door, kneel in earnest prayer, and then curl up in a chair and meditate, contemplate, search the scriptures, and cry out again and again in my heart, completely focusing my mind on the mind and will and presence of God until I can see a clear picture of him. I like to think of him with loving, outstretched arms. With such a loving image, I begin to feel my connection with him and a confirmation of his love. Sometimes I may have to work at this for hours, for a significant portion of the day, or for several days.

Now, I can just hear you saying, "Pat, get real. I don't

have five minutes to do that, let alone an hour or two. I am exhausted now just trying to keep up with things." I know all about your life because it is my life, too. I am busy also, and I have been for as long as I can remember. I know what it is like to chauffeur teenagers, face the laundry, serve in the Church and in the community, and be married to one of the Lord's equally busy servants. But that has *everything* to do with the point I wish to make.

I realize that life has to go on and that you will not be able to pursue this heavenly communication in a completely uninterrupted way, but if it is a high priority and a fundamental goal in your life, you will find ways, early or late, to be with God. If the key to your car or your mortgage payment check or a child were lost, would you take time to find them? Wouldn't finding them provide the peace you needed to then go about your day? If God is lost in your life and you are not going to be strong or stable without him, can you be focused and fixed enough to find him?

If you believed that your earthly father could comfort any heartache, heal any illness, solve any problem, or just be with you through the crucibles of life, wouldn't you call to him constantly? I am just childish enough to believe that our Father in Heaven can bless us in all those ways. The price to be paid for this kind of communion is time and your best powers of concentration, but by that investment you may offset untold hours, days, weeks, and months of struggle or sorrow or pain.

For me, sometimes this communing with God has to be early in the morning—that is my best time—when I am fresh and revelation is strong. Occasionally it has to be at night before I go to bed. In any case, it has to be when things are still, when the house is quiet and my mind is calm. I have the good fortune on those early mornings or late nights to have an unobstructed view of the beautiful Bountiful Temple just three-quarters of a mile from my home. As I look at the temple I see first its holiness, its brightness, beauty, and light. Whether rain or snow is falling, whether the clouds are low and hovering or the sun is bright overhead, the temple is lovely and firm. Its immovable quality steadies my soul—particularly on those days when I seem so very movable and so very drawn and driven in many directions. Its strong, straight spire reminds me that, unlike the temporal things in my life, my health, and the demands of the day and the laundry waiting to be done, the real me—the spiritual me, the real Pat Holland, the divine in me—is firm and fixed and stable and settled, like that temple on that hill. I take great comfort in the thought that the things that swirl around us are not us and that the demands on our lives are *not* life itself.

President Gordon B. Hinckley has spoken often of

meditation. My husband has commented on how often, in speaking to the First Presidency and the Quorum of the Twelve, he has asked that they make sure they take time for thoughtfulness, for pondering, for introspection, for meditation. He often refers to a statement of President David O. McKay: "Meditation is the language of the soul. It is defined as 'a form of private devotion, or spiritual exercise, consisting in deep, continued reflection on some religious theme'" (in Conference Report, April 1946, 113).

Somewhere in our lives there must be time and room for such personal communion. Somewhere in our lives there must be time and room for the celestial realities we say we believe in—or when will millennial peace be ours?

The kind of contemplation, reflection, and yearning for God I am speaking of can't be accomplished very handily in competition with cellular phones, computers, or a blaring TV. God can enter our realm only at our invitation. He stands at the door and knocks always, but someone has to hear that knock and let him enter. In this effort we ought to do whatever we can to make our houses—or our apartments or our condominiums—the temples, quite literally, that God intends them to be. Places for the Spirit of the Lord to dwell. Places for meditation, contemplation, prayer, and study. Places where good conversation and charity out of a pure heart can be present. Places where we find the fulness of God.

We need to simplify and spiritualize and celestialize. If most of what we are doing doesn't fit these categories, if at least some portion of our day is not turned to heaven, then we have a wrenching, rending emptiness awaiting us— isolation of the first order—and we will find no cloak of charity with which to protect ourselves or our sisters. We simply have to see what we can eliminate, what we can replace with something higher and holier, more reflective, compassionate, and eternal. Second only to dedicated temples, our homes are to be the sacred edifices of the Lord, places of peace and holiness and sanctity.

I am not being Pollyannish about this. I have already said that I know very well the demands upon a woman's time. It is because I know them so well that I am speaking as I am. I am speaking not only out of the depths of my heart but also out of the depths of my experience. You can say, "It can't be done. There is too much to do. It takes too much energy." Yes, you can say that—but you may miss forever the divine knock at the door. Or as the scripture says even more poignantly, "The harvest is past, the summer is [over], and [our souls are] not saved!" (D&C 56:16).

I believe a woman seeking the cloak of charity, a woman desiring with all her heart to receive the fulness of God, has a chance to break through these telestial, temporal trappings we hang onto. I believe she can find special powers, sacred powers, to bring to latter-day tasks. Through God she can receive the power to serve and sustain and sacrifice. Most of us are well acquainted with the responsibilities of service. I am sure many of you have baked cookies until your spatulas melted or baby-sat your neighbor's children until your brains sputtered. Occasionally when I am in such situations I fear my fatigue will slip into resentment, and then I wonder if being stretched so thin may not only prevent my developing new charity but actually diminish the supply I thought I had. I have learned, however, that though we may not have a completely willing heart every time we serve, such service molds our heart, blesses us, and does enlarge our capacity to give. We must remember, too, during periods of our lives in which we feel that all we can do is keep our own immediate circle of families or friends afloat, that *emotional and spiritual* service to others can sometimes be as important as physical acts.

My daughter, Mary, tells of being assigned to visit teach a friend but procrastinating the visit because her friend, who had three preschoolers and was pregnant with a fourth child, always seemed frazzled and frustrated. Mary knew she would want to shoulder some of her friend's tasks, but she also felt stretched to the limit with two preschoolers of her own, a husband in graduate school, and a demanding Church calling.

The idea of having three more children in her two-room apartment adding to her own children's chaos, even for only a few hours, seemed overwhelming. Yet, partially out of duty, but mostly out of love and a desire to lift her friend's spirits, she regularly offered to tend, clean house, and relieve her of some of her other burdens. Occasionally those offers were accepted; more often they were declined. Even when her friend accepted help, Mary could see little difference in her friend's mood.

One day, when Mary herself was having a particularly exasperating day, she called her friend—in the spirit of good visiting teaching—just to tell her that she couldn't help thinking of her and empathizing with her struggles. During that conversation, Mary sensed a gradual change in that sister's attitude, a kind of happiness she hadn't sensed in her very often.

Near the end of the conversation, her friend admitted to feeling nearly ecstatic to realize that Mary, who seemed to be able to handle everything with grace and goodwill, was having a miserable day. The sister explained, "Mary, I am so grateful. I've never had anyone share their frustrations with me. They are always terribly concerned about mine, and they just know I can't handle any others. Your honesty has made me feel so much better. I didn't think you ever felt frazzled like I do. I have always thought you were perfect. But today I see that you are not so different from me. Maybe I am doing just fine. I don't really need help as much as I just need to know that I am normal. Thanks!" Offering someone our companionship and our honest shared sorrows as well as joys is as important as quickly finishing a physical task for them.

What I wish to affirm is that we do need to charitably share and serve—emotionally and spiritually as well as temporally—but we must fill ourselves at the fountain of living water, at the feet of our Heavenly Father himself, or we have nothing of real strength to give. When we connect with God, then we will connect with others honestly and compassionately. When we pay the price to see God, we become aware of how closely connected we are to each other.

In the book of Revelation, John writes metaphorically of a woman representing the power and righteousness of the kingdom of God. When her life was endangered, she "fled into the wilderness" (Revelation 12:6). God had prepared a place for her, a place of safety and strength and protection. In dark and dangerous days, God will provide for us safe places, even wilderness places (I take that to mean sacred places undefiled by worldly civilization) where he protects us against evil and nourishes us with strength. Please allow yourself to take the time to go to that wilderness retreat now, that sanctuary, if you will—the temple, your own home, a place of privacy and revelation, a place filled with prayer and meditation and scriptural truths. Allow yourself to turn a few things down and turn a few things off. Seek to position yourself prayerfully in some solitude and serenity to receive the mind of God. Stop what you are so frantically doing and go into your private wilderness. Shut the door, turn out all earthly lights, set aside all earthly sights. Position yourself calmly and quietly in humble serenity until your prayer flows naturally and lovingly. When you feel God's presence, when you feel he is with you, you will be filled with a wonderful strength that will allow you to do anything in righteousness.

Thus filled and strengthened, we can return to the battle, to some inevitable noise and commotion and, yes, even some drudgery. But we do it more happily, more hopefully, more optimistically because we have communed with God and been filled with his joy, his charity, and his compassion, and we bear something of his light as we return. And because we are filled and strong, we can be a source of light, life, and love for others.

2

Meekness—A More Excellent Way

My daughter, Mary, as a freshman in college, was once troubled about her circumstance and felt very much alone. She was far away from us and all that seemed familiar. She needed sustaining strength and knew no mortal source from which to obtain it. She went to a private place to pray one night, and poured out her heart to God. She was so anxious, so concerned, and so much in need that the tears flowed freely down her cheeks.

Then, she said, in the midst of such fear, a remarkable moment came. Her head was bowed and her eyes full of tears. Her hands were clenched and extended well out in front of her. But she had the singular, startling sensation of one tear—just one—falling *not* down her cheeks but onto her fingertips, onto her hand out away from her bowed head. One tear seemingly shed from some other source. One tear, it seemed, shed from heaven.

"Mom, I know that really was my own tear," she later told me, "but it didn't seem like it was mine at the time. I felt as if it were a tear from the Savior himself, who was looking down on my prayer and on my aching heart and knowing exactly how I felt. I have never been more certain of our Father's love and the compassionate power of the redeeming sacrifice of his Son."

If an eighteen-year-old girl with all the world waiting ahead of her can feel such dramatic despair, my heart aches sincerely for the collective sorrow of the women of the world who so often seem to feel alone, unloved, unsuccessful, or even unredeemed. I suspect that for many of us—maybe all of us—regrets about past decisions, memories of unrequited love, sorrows for past mistakes, disappointments over failures, and anxieties about unfulfilled promises linger on in darkened minds and heavy hearts. If this in any way describes your current situation, I would have you know two things: (1) You are not alone; many people, including virtually *all* of the *very best people* I know, have had such feelings. (2) There is hope, there is a better way—"a more excellent way."

If my children have successfully taught me how to use the computer (a mighty big *if*), a word search on our LDS scripture software package indicates that the phrase "a more excellent way" appears twice in the scriptures. In both of those passages (1 Corinthians 12:31 and Ether 12:11), the phrase is associated with divine gifts—gifts of God's goodness that make possible "a more excellent way."

As I read these passages, I am struck with the variety and power of the gifts God is anxious to give us to help us live better, do better, and feel better. As my daughter found in her tear-filled moment of despair, and as I hope you have found at crucial moments in your life, of all the gifts that our Father in Heaven can bestow upon us, surely none is more needed than the peace that comes from the gift of his Son. Christ has warned that *in the world* we shall have tribulation, but he has also promised that *in Him* we shall have peace. I believe Longfellow captured a truth when he composed the following verse:

> *Let us then labour for an inward stillness—*
> *An inward stillness and an inward healing;*
> *That perfect silence, where the lips and heart*
> *Are still, and we no longer entertain*
> *Our own imperfect thoughts and vain opinions,*
> *But God alone speaks in us, and we wait*
> *In singleness of heart, that we may know*
> *His will, and in the silence of our spirits*
> *That we may do His will, and do that only.*

(Henry Wadsworth Longfellow, "Quiet Time," in *A Collection of Inspirational Verse for Latter-day Saints*, comp. Bryan B. Gardner and Calvin T. Broadhead [Bookcraft, 1963], 81)

We all long for that inner stillness—that perfect silence, free of imperfect thoughts and vain opinions—where God alone speaks to us. Christ and his love-filled sacrifice give us that opportunity. He asks of those whose lives are hurried and hyperactive, uncontrolled and uptight, fearful and frustrating, "[Do you want to] *run* about longer as a blind guide?" (D&C 19:40; emphasis added).

"[Or would you like to] *walk* in the meekness of my Spirit, and . . . have peace in me"? (D&C 19:23; emphasis added).

Is there any doubt about which of those options we would choose?

The word of God is unmistakable. Peace, and therefore "a more excellent way," will be found by walking in the meekness of his Spirit. Yet, if this is so, why do we often insist on continuing to run as blind guides?

For one thing, some of us may feel uncertain about the meaning of the phrase "walk in meekness." Does meekness seem vague and unattainable? The scriptures say so much about meekness, and yet I have heard many people ask things like: What does the Savior mean by meekness? How does one obtain it? How does one act who is meek? Does it mean giving over all your rights and privileges and becoming the human equivalent of cooked pasta—spineless and bland?

For many years now, I have asked similar questions myself. I have studied and prayed diligently for a very long time to find out what the answers may be. I do not think I have definitive answers for any of those questions, but I do feel that I know more now than I used to.

First, it is clear that meekness must have something to do with not desiring what God has willed for anyone else but desiring only what God has willed for me, Pat Holland. And I am convinced of, and thrilled by, the thought that God *has* a will, a plan for me personally, and a plan for each and every one of my brothers and sisters on this earth. I do believe deeply that God made each of us for an individually tailored and divine purpose. We each have a divine errand, and therein lies our joy. And while one purpose may seem more pleasant or important than another, this really is not so. All purposes are absolutely essential and important in the body of Christ. And all purposes lead to one thing: individual happiness.

Because that is true, I believe we will have peace to the degree that we are less envious of others' situations, less threatened by others' accomplishments, less concerned with others' progress, and more concerned with God's divine will for us.

As in all things, Jesus set the example for us in this matter. In his great intercessory prayer he stated, "I have glorified thee on the earth: I have finished the work which thou gavest *me* to do" (John 17:4; emphasis added).

If we are to use Christ as our guide through life, we too have to finish the work God has given *us* to do. I think Christ is trying to tell us simply and succinctly that complete joy will only be ours when our actions and aspirations match perfectly with God's plan for *us*, and not God's plan for somebody else.

Peace, joy, and happiness—a glorious heaven—will be out of reach on this earth unless we, as Christ taught, are true to the star God has set in the heavens just for us. Noted psychiatrist M. Scott Peck speaks of the mental anguish that occurs "when the conscious will of the individual deviates substantially from the will of God" (*The Road Less Traveled* [Simon and Schuster, 1978], n.p.).

A modern prophet validated this point when he wrote: "Do we realize that happiness here and now consists in freely, lovingly, joyfully acknowledging God's will for us—and doing it in all ways and all affairs big and small? To live perfectly is to live happily. To live happily is to grow in spiritual strength toward perfection. Every action performed in accord with God's will is part of that growth" (*Teachings of Ezra Taft Benson*, [Bookcraft, 1988], 339).

If meekness is to humbly live by God's will for us as individuals, there must be several practical implications for our behavior. Please indulge me as I share some very personal thoughts on what I consider manifestations of "walking in meekness."

The meek individual will be comfortable with the fact that God's timetable will be different for people who seem similarly situated. I have two loving, faithful, returned missionary sons. The youngest got engaged when he had been home from his mission roughly nine months. The oldest was still "anxiously engaged" in finding an eternal mate after he had been home roughly nine years. I love both of these boys with all my heart and equally so. It is hard to imagine, but knowing God's capacity for love to be much greater than my own, I must confess that he loves them even more than I do, and I know he does so with a perfect equality. Therefore, I do not believe for a moment that one was forgotten and the other remembered, that one deserved to be alone and the other to be in love, or that one was punished and the other blessed. I know that both of these righteous sons were somehow blessed equally. I don't know why two boys who seem so much alike should need such different timetables. But I do know—I had the divine reassurance—that both boys' lives are in the hands of God and that their particular situations were carefully, *not* capriciously, designed for their ultimate individual happiness. I believe, with all of my heart,

the same thing about every person who is living a faithful and obedient life.

Another way that I believe meekness is manifest in our lives is that we accept the fact that it is God's will that our individual human bodies come in different shapes and sizes. True, through exercise, diet, and dress we can and ought to conscientiously enhance what God has given us, as we would do with any gift we were given. However, this does not mean we have to become someone we physically are not. It's taken me a long time to realize this.

It is a slow suicide or at best a huge waste of time to try to be people we are not. Most women are not Julia Roberts. And most men are not Arnold Schwarzenegger (though I sense some think they are—after all these years my husband still instinctively flexes every time I take his arm). This leads to another point: The meek individual will accept and deal constructively, rather than critically, with the differences between the sexes. And let's face it, there are differences.

My husband and two sons are absolutely wonderful. But even I must confess that men are like artichokes. You have to work and work to peel off layer after layer before you get to the heart of the matter. In fairness, my patient and sensitive husband and sons tell me that they are convinced that when Werner Heisenberg developed the "uncertainty principle" of quantum physics, which asserts it is impossible to simultaneously know both the position and the speed of an object, that his units of analysis were not subatomic particles but LDS women. Rather than becoming bitter and incensed at what seems senseless in your opposite-sex family members and friends and acquaintances, look to see how those same weaknesses in one case may be strengths in another. Meekly acknowledge that you as well as they have certain proclivities that probably need to be moderated. Learn to enjoy the good things about the opposite sex.

Closely related to this point, the meek person will seek friendship and help in times of need in a peaceful, unfrenzied manner. The most difficult drowning victims to rescue are those who grab too tightly and desperately to their rescuers. When we are lonely and struggling, we must remember that our friends, our home teachers and bishops, and our family members are human. They have only so much time and strength. It is unfair and unmeek behavior to completely dominate their lives with our problems or even with our friendship.

However, it is also unmeek behavior to refuse help and friendship when it is needed. It is not God's will for us to stoically "go down with the ship" when rescuers are all around. I believe that the ability to say "I am hurting and need help" is a humble and courageous act of meekness.

Even Christ, when he was in agony, pleaded with his disciples to stay with him and pray with him, as he himself "prayed more earnestly" to his Father (Luke 22:44). If God himself can ask for help from friends, family, and priesthood leaders, undoubtedly we will not make it through life without doing the same.

So instead of giving up and sinking (by failing to ask for a blessing, or some time to talk, or a piece of counsel), and instead of dragging down with us those who have been sent to save us (by emotionally blackmailing our rescuers into giving us more time and emotional support than they genuinely have), we can become like a little child. More specifically, we can become like the little child of Scott Kelly, a bishop in Bowling Green, Ohio, who shared the following story:

"Years ago at a hotel swimming pool while vacationing as a family, my wife and I became distracted by the antics of our new baby. We turned back to the pool in horror to find that our 3-year-old son had walked off the last step of the pool into water over his head. He was standing with his head submerged and his arms raised and waving back and forth. I rushed over, grabbed his arms and pulled him out. He had been under water only a short time and was all right, but he said something that has since stayed with me. He said, 'I tried to cry under the water but I couldn't, so I held up my arms and waited because I *knew* you would come'" (*Church News*, 7 January 1995, 4).

If only we could remember, when the water of worldly sorrow and pressure is crashing in around us, that we don't need to give up, nor do we need to wildly thrash around strangling anything that looks like help. If we could just remember to peacefully hold out our arms to let people and God know we are hurting, the help will come. I promise it will come. If, as Mosiah says, we will "[become] as a little child, submissive, meek, [and] humble," we will soon find ourselves rescued and safely ensconced in a "blessed and happy state" (Mosiah 3:19; 2:41).

At this point, I can no longer avoid a question posed earlier. Does becoming like a child—submissive, meek, and humble—reduce us to having the personality and strength of a kettle of linguine? I certainly don't think so. In Numbers we are told that Moses "was very meek, above all the men which were upon the face of the earth" (Numbers 12:3). And Moses was anything but weak, opinionless, and timid. The Prophet Joseph adds this personal and helpful insight. It is recorded that he told some early Saints:

"Some of the company thought I was not a very meek Prophet; so I told them: 'I am meek and lowly in heart,' and will personify Jesus for a moment, to illustrate the principle, and [then] cried with a loud voice, 'Woe unto you, ye doctors; woe unto you, ye lawyers; woe unto you, ye scribes, Pharisees, and hypocrites!' But you cannot find the place where I ever went that I found fault with their food, their drink, their house, their lodgings; no, never; and this is what is meant by the meekness and lowliness of Jesus" (*Teachings of the Prophet Joseph Smith* [Deseret Book, 1976], 270).

I believe that what we learn from Moses and Joseph is that meekness also means strength—strength to be yourself, your best self, and to resist those people, principles, and places that work to abuse you physically, emotionally, and spiritually. I promise you that it is not God's will for you to be used and abused. Meekness means you must follow him where he will lead you, but he will always lead you away from, not toward, those who would fail to treat you with dignity and respect. It is still, and will always be, our Christian obligation to love, forgive, turn the other cheek, and not strike back at those who would treat us abusively. But that does not mean we have to willingly seek out and promote relationships with those who would harm our bodies, degrade our self-image, or undermine our faith. If you find yourself in such relationships I encourage you to meekly—which means with peaceful strength—insist that a change in behavior is required if the relationship is to continue.

These are just a few of the ways I feel meekness might

be demonstrated in our lives. But now I return to what I feel is the most important and central aspect of meekness. Deep in our spiritual conscience we know we were sent to earth to become instruments in God's hand as he orchestrates the finale of this last dispensation. When we are meek and in tune with our divine usefulness, playing our correct notes the best we can in harmony with the notes of our fellow players, I believe that we will feel at rest and that everything about us will fall together in a peaceful symphony of joy.

And I know that Christ wants us to have his fulness of joy. He wants us to have it *here* and *now*. This must be why in Alma 37 the Lord, who does not mince words, repeats himself. First he says, "Teach them to humble themselves and to be *meek and lowly in heart,*" and then again he says, "Teach them to never be weary of good works, but to be *meek and lowly in heart;* for such shall find rest to their souls" (Alma 37:33, 34; emphasis added).

You probably know that in the scriptures to "rest" means to enter into the fulness of God's glory (see D&C 84:24). God has promised us this glory, this beauty and peace, if we will walk in meekness. My understanding now, after prayer-fully pondering and earnestly seeking for several years, is that walking in meekness is simply walking with God: to be directed, prompted, and motivated by God and God alone, to avoid measuring life by our neighbors' or anyone else's yardstick.

God knows his children very well. He knows that the greatest threat to our meekness and peace is coveting, and that coveting ignites the motivation to act too often without his blessing. My mother has a very sweet, childlike faith. She always tried to teach me that when I saw a friend or neighbor who had more, did more, or was more than what I thought I could be, I was simply to remember: "Be still, and know that I am God" (Psalm 46:10; D&C 101:16).

It has taken me years with bouts of self-doubt over this or that to come to the point where I now trust God as my mother does.

Can *we*, by taking thought, add one cubit to our stature?

Can *we*, by taking thought, clothe ourselves greater than Solomon or the lilies of the field?

It's useless to worry about such things, because God, who knows our needs better than we do, will give us what we need. It's so much more peaceful to seek only the kingdom of God and let all other things be added unto us as necessary. It's so much more peaceful when we "Take . . . *no* thought for the morrow: [but let] the morrow . . . take thought for the things of itself" (Matthew 6:34; 3 Nephi 13:34; emphasis added).

When we covet, we are taking thought for the morrow,

and the next day, and the next day. That just leaves us all too dazed.

All of us will, from time to time, feel twinges of jealousy. We don't need to cast ourselves off into outer darkness or lacerate ourselves into immobility for having these feelings. It is part of our human nature. Listen to this translation of James 4:5 from the New English Bible: "Do you suppose that Scripture has no meaning when it says that the spirit which God implanted in man turns toward envious desires? And yet the grace he gives us is stronger." That means that although any of us may feel that twinge of jealousy, God's grace can help us transcend that feeling.

One way for us to move away from envy and covetousness would be to ask for God's grace the minute we feel the first tiny, tiny flutter of jealousy. He alone can dissolve vain ambitions. He alone can sanctify and purify those thoughts. God's hand pulls us away from the painful path of coveting to a meek and more peaceable walk with him if we truly desire that help.

The Savior pleads for us to pray in such circumstances: "Pray always, and I will pour out my Spirit upon you, and great shall be your blessing—yea, *even more* than if you should obtain treasures of earth" (D&C 19:38; emphasis added).

I testify that prayer is a most powerful path to meekness

and gentleness and peace. I testify that the greatest joy I know is when I am not just praying on my knees or in my closet or secret hiding place but when I am praying constantly in my heart. Not all of our prayers are answered as directly and positively as we might want. But every answer—or lack of answer—from the Lord is such that it will lead to greener pastures. This gospel is filled with promises, and I am grateful for them all.

I hope that you recognize and believe in the promises; there is a green pasture for each and every one of us. And do not be deceived into thinking that even though there are different and seemingly unfair paths in life, that in the end we all get the same pasture. Your pasture will compensate for your path, and my pasture will compensate for my path. Whether in this life or the next, and it is always in both, when the Lord opens up the windows of heaven, there will be a pouring forth of blessings that directly heal and repay for every individual pain and sacrifice you are experiencing. He will throw open those windows for every child who simply has enough faith to obey and believe that he is good.

Believe me when I tell you that God is a God of goodness, mercy, and justice. Ultimately, he cannot treat his righteous children differently. Whatever blessings you have gone without will be made up to you in divine and glorious fashion. I give you every assurance, they will be made up to you to the point where you will not be confident that God treated you fairly but embarrassed that he treated you so very generously.

There have been times in my spiritual life when I have felt as settled and immovable as the rock of Gibraltar. And then comes an upheaval, a mighty change. Sometimes the upheaval comes from outside circumstances, and sometimes it comes from within. Often it comes just when I'm feeling that my weaknesses are forgiven, that they are finally becoming strengths, just when I feel my current opportunities for service have put me right before the Lord. That is when it seems the Lord chooses to shift my circumstances, and everything seems to tumble around me like a large set of dominoes.

At those times, my first thought is often, "He is angry with me. What have I done wrong? What sin did I commit? Why have I been moved out of my comfort zone, and how can I get back in it?" But I am getting older now—we all do that—and I am growing out of those reactions. I am not seeing God's stretching of me as punishment but as reward because it has always led me on to a higher level of spiritual understanding and always—always!—has brought me unanticipated and seemingly unearned blessings.

It isn't God's anger that allows change and upheaval

and, from time to time, suffering in our lives. It is in fact his tenderest love that allows it. Through all of this I am learning that God doesn't want me to take much notice of external things, doesn't want me to try to find rest in outward circumstances and the vanities of the world. We are forced to keep looking beyond those, especially when they disappoint us or let us down. We are forced to keep looking to him.

God does not equate peace with worldly prosperity or success. That kind of prosperity—financial, emotional, or otherwise—can crumble like a house built on sand. Those are false resting places. God in his infinite love—if we will be meek enough to receive him and his plan for us—lifts us as though we were in the palm of his hand and places us in that permanent peace that comes only in and through the love of God.

The road to meekness and peace is long and it can be lonely, but it is the road to God. Nineteenth-century evangelist Hannah Whitall Smith wrote: "When the fig tree ceases to blossom, and there is no fruit in the vines; when the labor of the olive shall fail, and the fields shall yield no meat; when the flock shall be cut off from the fold, and there shall be no herd in the stalls, then, and often not until then, will our souls learn to rejoice in the Lord only."

This is so because *only* "in the gift of his Son, hath God prepared a more excellent way" (Ether 12:11).

Let yourself *fall* upon the grace and gift of the Son of God. Let your hand fall into his hand that he may lead you. Want his companionship over any other joy in this world. Desire to do the work he sent you here to do. May we all do so, and thus find a more excellent way in the peace that surpasseth understanding.

3

"But One Thing Is Needful"

Just after my release from the general presidency of the Young Women in April 1986, I had the opportunity of spending a week in Israel. It had been a very difficult and demanding two years for me. Being a good mother, with the ample amount of time needed to succeed at that task, had always been my first priority, so I had tried to be a full-time mother to a grade-schooler, a high-schooler beginning to date, and a son preparing for his mission. I had also tried to be a full-time wife to a staggeringly busy university president with all of the twenty-four-hours-a-day campus responsibility that could be required of both of us at a place like Brigham Young University. And I had tried to be as much of a full-time counselor in that general presidency as one living fifty miles from the office could be. Sister Ardeth Kapp and the others were wonderfully patient with me. I will never be able to thank Ardeth enough. But in an important period of forming principles and starting programs for the Young Women, I worried that I wasn't doing enough—and I tried to run a little faster.

Toward the end of my two-year term, my health was going downhill. I was losing weight steadily and couldn't seem to do anything to halt that. Furthermore, I wasn't sleeping well. My husband and children were trying to bandage me together even as I was trying to do the same for them. We were exhausted. And yet, I kept wondering what I might have done to manage it all better. The Brethren, always compassionate, were watching and at the end of the two years extended a loving release. As grateful as my family and I were for the conclusion of my term of service, I nevertheless felt a loss of association—and, I confess, some loss of identity—with these women whom I had come to love so much. Who was I and where was I in this welter of demands? Should life be as hard as all this? How successful had I been in my several and competing assignments? Or had I muffed them all? The days after my release were about as difficult as the weeks before it. I didn't have any reserve to call on. My tank was on empty, and I wasn't sure there was a filling station anywhere in sight.

It was just a few weeks later that my husband had the assignment in Jerusalem to which I have referred, and the Brethren traveling on the assignment requested that I accompany him. "Come on," he said. "You can recuperate in the Savior's land of living water and bread of life." As weary as I was, I packed my bags, believing—or, at the very least, hoping—that the time there would be a healing respite.

On a pristinely clear and beautifully bright day, I sat overlooking the Sea of Galilee and reread Luke 10:38–42. But instead of the words there on the page, I thought I saw with my mind and heard with my heart these words: "Pat, Pat, thou art careful and troubled about many things." Then the power of pure and personal revelation seized me as I read, "But one thing [only one thing] is truly needful."

In Israel in May the sun is so bright that you feel as if you are sitting on top of the world. I had just visited the spot in Bethoron where the "sun stood still" for Joshua (see Joshua 10:13), and indeed on that day it seemed so for me as well. As I sat pondering my problems, I felt that same sun's healing rays like warm liquid pouring into my heart— relaxing, calming, and comforting my troubled soul. I found myself lifted to a higher view of my life.

Spirit to spirit, our loving Father in Heaven seemed to be whispering to me, "You don't have to worry over so many things. The one thing that is needful—the only thing that is truly needful—is to keep your eyes toward the sun—my Son." "Learn of me," he seemed to say, "and listen to my words; walk in the meekness of my Spirit, and you shall have peace in me" (D&C 19:23). Suddenly I did have peace. I knew, as surely as I have ever known anything, that my life had always been in his hands—from the very beginning! And so is the life of every woman who wants to do right and grows in capacity and tries to give all she can. The sea lying peacefully before my very eyes had been tempest tossed and dangerous many, many times. All I needed to do was to renew my faith and get a firm grasp of his hand, and together we could walk on the water.

We all at one time or another find ourselves in the midst of a turbulent sea. There are times when we, too, would like to cry out, "Master, carest thou not that we perish?" (Mark 4:38).

I would like to pose a question for each of us to ponder. How do we as women make that quantum leap from being troubled and worried, even about legitimate concerns, to exercising even greater faith? One frame of mind surely seems to negate the other. Faith and fear cannot long coexist. While you think of faith and walking hand in hand with God, I would like to examine why I believe there are so many worries—"troubles," Luke 10:41 calls them—and to note some of the things we are legitimately worried about.

I have served as a Relief Society president in four different wards. Two of those wards were for single women, and two were more traditional wards with many young mothers. As I sat in counsel with my single sisters, my heart often ached as they described to me their feelings of loneliness and disappointment. They felt that their lives had no meaning or purpose in a church that rightly puts so much emphasis on marriage and family life. Most painful of all was the occasional suggestion that their singleness was their own fault—or worse yet, a selfish desire. They were anxiously seeking for peace and purpose, something of real value to which they could give their lives.

Yet at the very same time, it seemed to me that the young mothers had easily as many concerns. They described to me the struggles of trying to raise children in an increasingly difficult world, of never having enough time or means or freedom to feel like a person of value because they were always stretched to the ragged edge of survival. And there were so few tangible evidences that what they were doing was really going to be successful. There was no one to give them a raise in pay and, beyond their husbands (who may or may not have remembered to do it), no one to compliment them on a job well done. And they were always tired! The one thing I remember so vividly with these young mothers was that they were always so tired.

Then there were those women who through no fault of their own found themselves the sole providers for their families financially, spiritually, emotionally, and in every other way. I could not even comprehend the challenges they faced. Obviously, in some ways theirs was the most demanding circumstance of all.

The perspective I have gained over these many years of listening to the worries of women is that no one woman or group of women—single, married, divorced, or widowed, homemakers or professionals—has cornered the full market on concerns. There seem to be plenty of challenges to go around—and, I hasten to add, marvelous blessings as well. Every one of us does have privileges and blessings, and we do have fears and trials, ranging from loneliness to child rearing to inactive husbands to physical health and self-esteem.

It seems bold to say, but common sense suggests that never before in the history of the world have women, including Latter-day Saint women, been faced with greater complexity in their concerns. In addressing these concerns I am very appreciative of the added awareness that the women's movement has given to a gospel principle we have had since Mother Eve and before—that of agency, the right to choose.

But one of the most unfortunate side effects we have faced in this matter of agency is that because of the increasing diversity of lifestyles for women of today, we seem even more uncertain and less secure with each other. We are getting not closer but further away from that sense of community and sisterhood that has sustained us and given us unique strength for generations. There seems to be an increase in our competitiveness and a decrease in our generosity with one another.

Those who have the time and energy to can their fruits and vegetables develop a great skill that will serve them well in time of need—and in our uncertain economic times, that could be almost any day of the week. But they shouldn't look down their noses at those who buy their peaches, or who don't like zucchini in any of the thirty-five ways there are to disguise it, or who have simply made a conscious choice to use their time and energy in some other purposeful way.

And where am I in all of this? For three-fourths of my life I was threatened to the core because I hated to sew. Now I *can* sew; if absolutely forced to, I *will* sew—but I hate it. Imagine my burden over the last twenty-five or thirty years, faking it in Relief Society sessions and trying to smile when six little girls walk into church all pinafored and laced and ribboned and petticoated—identical, hand sewn—all trooping ahead of their mother, who has the same immaculate outfit. Competitive? I wanted to tear their pleats out.

I don't necessarily consider it virtuous, lovely, or of good report, or praiseworthy—but I'm honest in my antipathy toward sewing. If even one sister out there is weeping tears of relief, then I consider my public shame at least a partial blow against stereotyping. I have grown up a little since those days in at least two ways—I now genuinely admire a mother who can do that for her children, and I have ceased feeling guilty that sewing is not particularly rewarding to me.

We simply cannot call ourselves Christian and continue to judge one another—or ourselves—so harshly. No Mason jar of Bing cherries is worth a confrontation that robs us of our compassion and our sisterhood.

Obviously the Lord has created us with different personalities, as well as differing degrees of energy, interest, health, talent, and opportunity. So long as we are committed to living righteously and with faithful devotion, we should celebrate these divine differences, knowing they are a gift from God. We must not feel so frightened; we must not be so threatened and insecure; we must not need to find exact replicas of ourselves in order to feel validated as women of worth. There are many things over which we can be divided, but one thing is needful for our unity—the empathy and compassion of the living Son of God.

I was married in 1963, the very year Betty Friedan published her society-shaking book, *The Feminine Mystique*, so as an adult woman I can look back with only childhood memories of the gentler forties and fifties. But it must have

been much more comfortable to have a pattern already prepared for you and neighbors on either side whose lives gave
you role models for your own. However, it must have been
that much more painful for those who, through no fault of
their own, were single then, or who had to work, or who
struggled with broken families. Now, with our increasingly
complex world, even that earlier model is torn, and we seem
to be even less sure of who we are and where we are going.

Surely there has not been another time in history in
which women have questioned their self-worth as harshly
and critically as in the second half of the twentieth century.
Many women are searching almost frantically for a sense of
personal purpose and meaning—and many Latter-day Saint
women are searching, too, for eternal insight and meaning
in their femaleness.

If I were Satan and wanted to destroy a society, I think I
would stage a full-blown blitz on its women. I would keep
them so distraught and distracted that they would never find
the calming strength and serenity for which their sex has
always been known. He has effectively done that, catching
us in the crunch of trying to be superhuman instead of real-
istically striving to reach our individual purpose and unique
God-given potential within such diversity. He tauntingly
teases us that if we don't have it all—fame, fortune, families, and fun—and have it every minute all the time, we

have been short-changed; we are second-class citizens in the race of life. You'd have to be deaf, dumb, and blind not to get these messages in today's world, and as a sex we are struggling, our families are struggling, and our society struggles. Drugs, teenage pregnancies, divorce, family violence, and suicide are some of the ever-increasing side effects of our collective life in the express lane.

As a result, we are experiencing new and undiagnosed stress-related illnesses. The Epstein-Barr syndrome, for one, has come into our popular medical jargon. Its symptoms are low-grade fevers, aching joints, and other flulike symptoms—but it isn't the flu. It carries with it overwhelming exhaustion, muscular weakness, and physical debilitations—but it isn't the dreaded AIDS. Its victims are often confused and forgetful—but, no, it isn't Alzheimer's. Many feel suicidal, but this disease lacks the traditional characteristics of clinical depression. And yes, it can strike men, but three times out of four it doesn't. This illness is primarily a women's disease, and those most vulnerable are the so-called "fast-track" women in high-stress, conflicting roles (see "Malaise of the '80s," *Newsweek*, 27 October 1986, 105).

When I mentioned this to the young women in the BYU student body, I was flooded with telephone calls and letters saying, "I have it! I have it! I must have

Epstein-Barr!" Well, whether they do or do not, I can't say. But the body and its immune system are affected by stress. Those calls and letters tell me that too many are struggling and suffering; too many are running faster than they have strength, expecting too much of themselves. We must have the courage to be imperfect while striving for perfection. We must not allow our own guilt, or the feminist books, or the talk-show hosts, or the whole media culture to sell us a bill of goods—or rather, a bill of no goods.

I believe we can become so sidetracked in our compulsive search for identity and self-esteem and self-awareness that we really believe it can be found in having perfect figures or academic degrees or professional status or even absolute motherly success. Yet in so searching externally, we can be torn from our true internal, eternal selves. We often worry so much about pleasing and performing for others that we lose our own uniqueness—that full and relaxed acceptance of ourselves as persons of worth and individuality. We become so frightened and insecure that we cannot be generous toward the diversity and the individuality and, yes, the problems, of our neighbors. Too many women with these anxieties watch helplessly as their lives unravel from the very core that centers and sustains them. Too many are like a ship at sea without sail or rudder, tossed to and fro (as the

Apostle Paul said) until more and more are genuinely, rail-grabbingly seasick.

Where is the sureness that allows us to sail our ship whatever winds may blow—with the master seaman's triumphant cry, "Steady as she goes"? Where is the inner stillness we so cherish and for which our sex traditionally has been known?

I believe we can find it—the steady footing and the stilling of the soul—by turning away from the fragmentation of physical preoccupations, or superwoman accomplishments, or endless popularity contests, and returning instead to the wholeness of our soul, that unity in our very being that balances the demanding and inevitable diversity of life.

One woman who is not of our faith but whose writings I love is Anne Morrow Lindbergh. In commenting on the female despair and general torment of our times, she writes: "The Feminists did not look . . . far [enough] ahead; they laid down no rules of conduct. For them it was enough to demand the privileges. . . . And [so] woman today is still searching. We are aware of our hunger and needs, but still ignorant of what will satisfy them. With our garnered free time, we are more apt to drain our creative springs than to refill them. With our pitchers, we attempt . . . to water a field, [instead of] a garden. We throw ourselves indiscriminately into committees and causes. Not knowing how to free the spirit, we try to muffle its demands in distractions. Instead of stilling the center, the axis of the wheel, we add more centrifugal activities to our lives—which tend to throw us [yet more] off balance.

"Mechanically we have gained, in the last generation, but spiritually we have . . . lost."

She emphasizes, "[For women] the problem is [still] how to feed the soul" (*Gift from the Sea*, 20th anniversary edition, with an afterword by the author [Vintage Books, 1978], 51–52).

I have pondered long and hard about the feeding of our inner self, of the "one thing needful" amidst too many troublesome things. It is no coincidence that we speak of feeding the spirit just as we would speak of feeding the body. We need constant nourishment for both. The root word *hale* (as in "hale and hearty") is the common root to words like *whole*, *health*, *heal*, and *holy*. President Ezra Taft Benson taught: "There is no question that the health of the body affects the spirit, or the Lord would never have revealed the Word of Wisdom. God has never given any temporal commandments—that which affects our bodies also affects our souls" (*Come unto Christ* [Deseret Book, 1983], 33). We need so much for body, mind, and spirit to come together, to unite in one healthy, stable soul.

Surely God is well balanced, so perhaps we are just that

much closer to him when we are. In any case, I like the link between *hale, whole, health, heal,* and *holy.* Our unity of soul within diversity of circumstance—our "stilling of the center"—is worth any effort that may encourage it.

As I noted previously, I believe we make too many external quests seeking peace or fulfillment. Only rarely do we consider the glorious possibility within us, within our own souls. We seem never to remember that divine promise, "The kingdom of God is within you" (Luke 17:21). Perhaps we forget that the Kingdom of God is within us because too much attention is given to the Kingdom of Women outside us, this outer shell, this human body of ours, and the frail, too-flimsy world in which it moves. So, as women of faith, we should make an inward quest.

In my contribution to this effort, may I share with you my own analogy of something I read years ago, a process that helped me then and helps me still—in my examination of inner strength and spiritual growth.

The analogy is of a soul—a human soul, with all of its splendor—being placed in a beautifully carved but very tightly locked box. Reigning in majesty and illuminating our soul in this innermost box is our Lord and our Redeemer, Jesus Christ, the living Son of the living God. This box is then placed—and locked—inside another larger one, and so on until five beautifully carved but very securely locked boxes await the woman who is skillful and wise enough to open them. In order for her to have free communication with the Lord she must find the keys to these boxes and unlock their contents. Success will then reveal to her the beauty and divinity of her own soul, her gifts and her grace as a daughter of God.

For me, prayer is the key to the first box. We kneel to ask help for the tasks and then arise to find that the first lock is now open. But this ought not to seem just a convenient and contrived miracle. No, if we are to search for real light and eternal certainties, we have to pray as the ancients prayed. We are women now, not children, and are expected to pray with maturity. The words most often used to describe urgent, prayerful labor are *wrestle*, *plead*, *cry*, and *hunger*. In some sense, prayer may be the hardest work we will ever be engaged in, and perhaps it should be. We sing, "Prayer is the soul's sincere desire" (*Hymns*, no. 145), and our most basic declaration is that we have no other God before our Father in Heaven. Prayer is our most pivotal protection against overinvolvement in worldly things, against becoming so absorbed with possessions and privilege and honors and status that we no longer desire to undertake the search for our soul.

Those who, like Enos, pray in faith and gain entrance to a new dimension of their divinity are led to box number two. Here our prayers alone do not seem to be sufficient. We must turn to the scriptures for God's long-recorded teachings about our soul. We must learn. Surely every woman in this Church is under divine obligation to learn and grow and develop. We are God's diverse array of unburnished talents, and we must not bury these gifts or hide our light. If the glory of God is intelligence, then learning stretches us toward him, especially learning from the scriptures. There he uses many metaphors for divine influence, such as "living water" (John 4:10) and "the bread of life" (John 6:35).

I have discovered that if my own progress stalls, it stalls from malnutrition, born of not eating and drinking daily from his holy writ. There have been challenges in my life that would have completely destroyed me, would have precluded any spiritual progression at all, had I not had a copy of the scriptures by my bed and a small set in my purse so that I could partake of them day and night at a moment's notice. Meeting God in scripture has been like a divine intravenous feeding for me—a celestial I.V. that my son once described as an "angelical cord." So box two is opened spirit to spirit through the scriptures. I have discovered that by opening them I have opened it. There I can have, again and again, an exhilarating encounter with God.

At the beginning of such success in emancipating the soul, however, Lucifer becomes more anxious, especially as we approach box number three. He knows something is coming, one very important and fundamental principle. He knows that we are about to learn that to truly find ourselves we must lose ourselves, so he begins to block our increased efforts to love—love God, love our neighbor, and love ourselves. Remember, the Lord has asked above all else that we love. Everything else we do is secondary, and in fulfilling the two great commandments we can often measure how much we love the Lord by how well we truly love our neighbor. I firmly believe that if we did nothing else but faithfully practice love for our neighbor, we would have found our ability and success in accomplishing all else. Yet Satan's skillful deception has been to obscure this chance for near success. He has, especially in the last decade, enticed the people of the world to engage their energies in the pursuit of romantic love or thing-love or excessive self-love. In so doing, they can forget that appropriate self-love and self-esteem are the promised rewards for putting other things first. "Whosoever shall seek to save his life shall lose it; and whosoever shall lose his life shall preserve it" (Luke 17:33). Box three opens only with the key of charity.

Real growth and genuine insight are coming now. But the lid to box four seems nearly impossible to penetrate, for we are climbing, too, in this story, and the way inward is also the way upward. Unfortunately the faint-hearted and fearful often turn back here—the going seems too difficult, the lock too secure. This is a time for self-evaluation. To see ourselves as we really are often brings pain, but it is only through true humility that we will come to know God. Our Savior admonishes, "Learn of me; for I am meek and lowly in heart" (Matthew 11:29). We must be patient with ourselves as we overcome weaknesses, and we must remember to rejoice over all that is good in us. This will strengthen the inner woman and leave her less dependent on outward acclaim.

When the soul reaches the stage where it pays less attention to praise, it then also cares very little when the public disapproves. Comparing and competition and jealousy and envy begin to have no meaning now. Just imagine the powerful spirit that would exist in our female society if we finally arrived at the point where, like our Savior, our real desire was to be counted as the least among our sisters. The rewards here are of such profound strength and quiet triumph of faith that we are carried into an even brighter sphere. So the fourth box, unlike the others, is broken open, as a heart and contrite spirit are broken. Or better yet, it bursts open as a flower blooms and the earth is reborn. We too are reborn in humility and repentance and renewal. We are born of water and of fire. We are born of the Spirit of God.

To share with you my feelings of opening the fifth box, I must compare the beauty of our souls with the holiness of our temples. There, in a setting not of this world, in a place where fashions and position and professions go unrecognized, we have our chance to meet God face-to-face. For those who, like the brother of Jared, have the courage and faith to break through the veil into that sacred center of existence, we will find the brightness of the final box brighter than the noonday sun. There we will find peace and serenity and stillness that will anchor our souls forever, for there we will find God. Wholeness. Holiness. That is what it says over the entrance to the fifth box: "Holiness to the Lord." "Know ye not that ye are the temple of God?" (1 Corinthians 3:16). I testify that you are holy—that divinity is abiding within you waiting to be uncovered, to be unleashed and magnified and demonstrated.

I believe that if any woman is to find her own personal identity and value for herself, her family, her society, and her God, she will have to uncover her own soul and set it free. Then it can and should range throughout all eternity, having great influence and doing much good.

As I conclude by trying to articulate what I feel about this whole matter of identity—the eternal identity of our womanhood—I wish to stress that these thoughts are my

⌣..n, and I take full responsibility for them. Above all, I do not want them to be misunderstood or to give offense.

I have heard it said by some that the reason women in the Church struggle somewhat to know themselves is that they don't have a divine female role model. But we do believe we have a mother in heaven. May I quote from President Spencer W. Kimball in a general conference address: "When we sing that doctrinal hymn . . . 'O My Father,' we get a sense of the ultimate in maternal modesty, of the restrained, queenly elegance of our Heavenly Mother, and knowing how profoundly our mortal mothers have shaped us here, do we suppose her influence on us as individuals to be less?" (*Ensign*, May 1978, 6).

I have never questioned why our mother in heaven seems veiled to us, for I believe the Lord has his reasons for revealing as little as he has on that subject. Furthermore, I believe we know much more about our eternal nature than we think we do, and it is our sacred obligation to identify it and to teach it to our young sisters and daughters. In so doing, we can strengthen their faith and help them through the counterfeit confusions of these difficult latter days. Let me point out some examples.

The Lord has not placed us in this lone and dreary world without a blueprint for living. In Doctrine and Covenants 52:14 we read, "And again, I will give unto you a pattern in *all things, that ye may not be deceived"* (emphasis added). He certainly includes us as women in that promise. He has given us patterns in the Bible, the Book of Mormon, the Doctrine and Covenants, the Pearl of Great Price; and he has given us patterns in the temple ceremony.

As we study these patterns we must continually ask, "Why does the Lord choose to say these particular words and present it in just this way?" We know he uses metaphors and symbols and parables and allegories to teach us of his eternal ways. For example, we all have recognized the relationship between Abraham and Isaac that so parallels God's anguish over the sacrifice of his Son, Jesus Christ. But, as women, do we stretch ourselves and also ask about Sarah's travail in this experience as well? We could, and if we did, I believe we would learn. We need to search, and we need always to look for deeper meaning. We should look for parallels and symbols. We should look for themes and motifs just as we would in a Bach or a Mozart composition, and we should look for patterns—repeated patterns—in the gospel.

One obvious pattern is that both the Bible and the Book of Mormon start off with family, including family conflict. I have always believed that symbolized something eternal about all of us as "family" far more than the story of just those particular parents or those particular children. Surely all of us—married or single, with children and without—see something of Adam and Eve and something of Cain and Abel every day of our lives. With or without marriage or with or without children, surely we have some of the feelings of Lehi, Sariah, Laman, Nephi, Ruth, Naomi, Esther, the sons of Helaman, and the daughters of Ishmael.

Those are types and shadows for us, prefigurations of our own mortal joys and sorrows, just as Joseph and Mary are, in a sense, types and shadows of parental devotion as they nurtured the Son of God himself, with Mary playing the principal mortal role. These all seem to me to be symbols of higher principles and truths, symbols carefully chosen to show us the way, whether we are married or single, young or old, with family or without.

And obviously the temple is highly symbolic. May I share an experience I had there once? It has to do with the careful choice of words and symbols. I have chosen my own words carefully so that nothing I say will be improperly shared outside the temple. My only quotations are taken from published scripture.

Maybe it was coincidence, but as someone has said, "Coincidence is a small miracle in which God chooses to remain anonymous." In any case, as I waited in the temple chapel, I sat next to a very elderly man who unexpectedly but sweetly turned to me and said, "If you want a clear picture of the Creation, read Abraham, chapter 4." As I started

to turn to Abraham, I just happened to brush past Moses
3:5: "For I, the Lord God, created all things, of which I have
spoken, spiritually, before they were naturally upon the face
of the earth." Another message of prefiguration again—a
spiritual pattern giving meaning to mortal creations. I then
read Abraham 4 carefully and took the opportunity of going
to an initiatory session. I left there with greater revelatory
light on something I'd always known in my heart to be so—
that men and women are joint heirs of the blessings of
the priesthood and, even though men bear the greater burden of administering it, women are not without their
priesthood-related responsibilities also.

Then as I attended the endowment session, I asked
myself if I were the Lord and could give my children on
earth only a simplified but powerfully symbolic example of
their roles and missions, how much would I give and where
would I start? I listened to every word. I watched for patterns and prototypes.

I quote to you from Abraham 4:27: "So the Gods went
down to organize man in their own image, in the image of
the Gods to form they him, male *and* female to form they
them" (emphasis added). They formed male, and they
formed female—in the image of the Gods, in their own
image.

Then in a poignant exchange with God, Adam stated

57

that he would call the woman "Eve." And why did he call her Eve? "Because she was the mother of all living" (Genesis 3:20; Moses 4:26).

As I tenderly acknowledge the very real pain that many single women, or married women who have not borne children, feel about any discussion of motherhood, could we consider this one possibility about our eternal female identity—our unity in our diversity. Eve was given the identity of the mother of all living—years, decades, perhaps centuries before she had ever borne a child. It would appear that her motherhood preceded her maternity just as surely as the perfection of the Garden preceded the struggles of mortality. I believe *mother* is one of those very carefully chosen words, one of those words rich with meaning after meaning after meaning. We must not, at all costs, let that word divide us. I believe with all my heart that it is first and foremost a statement about our nature, not a head count of our children. I have only three children and have wept that I could not have eight. (Some of you may have eight and weep that you can't have three.) And I know that some of you without any have wept too. And sometimes, too many have simply been angry over the very subject itself. For the sake of our eternal motherhood I plead that this not be so.

Some women give birth and raise children but never "mother" them. Others, whom I love with all my heart, "mother" all their lives but have never given birth. Therefore, we must understand that however we accomplish it, parenthood is the highest of callings, the holiest of assignments. And all of us are Eve's daughters, married or single, maternal or barren, every one of us. We are created in the image of the Gods to become gods and goddesses. And we can provide something of that divine pattern, that maternal prototype, for each other and for those who come after us. Whatever our circumstance, we can reach out, touch, hold, lift, and nurture—but we cannot do it in isolation. We need a community of sisters stilling the soul and binding the wounds of fragmentation.

I know that God loves us individually and collectively—as women—and that he has a personal mission, an individual purpose for every one of us. As I learned on my Galilean hillside, I testify that if our desires are righteous, God overrules for our good and will tenderly attend to our needs. In our diversity and individuality, my prayer is that we will be united—united in seeking our specific, foreordained mission, united in asking, not "What can the kingdom do for me?" but "What can I do for the kingdom? How do I fulfill the measure of *my* creation? In my circumstances and my challenges and with my faith, where is my *full* realization of the godly image in which I was created?"

With faith in God, his prophets, his Church, and

ourselves—faith in our own divine creation—may we be peaceful and let go of our cares and troubles over so many things. May we believe—nothing doubting—in the light that shines, even in a dark place.

We are the Lord's disciples. He accepts us as we are, even as we are growing toward what we must become. Rest in that love. Bathe and luxuriate in it. Let it relax, calm, and comfort you. Let us keep our face to the Son and come unto him.

4

The Things of a Better World

In 1830, the Lord offered simple but essential counsel to Emma Smith that would serve any person who is searching for a quiet heart. "Thou shalt lay aside the things of this world," he said, "and seek for the things of a better" (D&C 25:10). My prayer for each of us is that we may lay aside the things of this world, and seek for the things—including the peace and tranquillity and hope and serenity—of a better world. I believe that inherent in that quest is the joy we all seek as women and the promise of "peace in this world, and eternal life in the world to come" (D&C 59:23).

It is as the Savior himself told his disciples: "Take no thought for your life, what ye shall eat, or what ye shall drink; nor yet for your body, what ye shall put on" (Matthew 6:25). He told them not to worry about "things," about so much that is so temporal—you know, what am I going to wear and I hope they notice my nails. If the Savior had been speaking in our day and time rather than in Jerusalem in the meridian of time, he might simply have said, "Be peaceful. Be believing. Live close to God. And let go of trying to keep

up with the Joneses." "Is not the life more than meat, and the body than raiment?" he asked. In almost these terms he said, "You are silly to spend so much time worrying about temporal and often petty things because you can't do very much about them anyway." Now, that is my loose translation of what he said. What he *really* said was, "Which of you by taking thought [or by worrying about it] can add one cubit unto his [or her] stature?" (Matthew 6:27). Why waste time worrying that we are 4' 11" and, well, "solid" when we would like to be 5' 9" and slinky? These are the wrong concerns about the wrong things because they are things we can't change.

As a preface to that counsel, the Savior had just said, "Lay not up for yourselves treasures upon earth, where moth and rust doth corrupt, and where thieves break through and steal: But lay up for yourselves treasures in heaven . . . for where your treasure is, there will your heart be also." And then this powerful directive: "No man [or woman] can serve two masters; for either [she] will hate the one, and love the other; or else [she] will hold to the one, and despise the other. Ye cannot serve God and mammon" (Matthew 6:19–21, 24).

The Savior made special space for these few precious words in his Sermon on the Mount, perhaps the most important sermon ever uttered in the history of the world, and I believe them with all my heart. If this kind of counsel mattered there and then, maybe it still matters here and now. I add my conviction to the Savior's knowledge and declaration that involving ourselves too emotionally and too often and too devotedly in these temporal and transitory issues in our lives keeps us from *real* life, from the real truth, from the sweet and nourishing rest God longs to deliver to our spiritual souls.

These are my own personal reflections on this matter. I don't claim to have been urged by any other special authority—even the one I am married to—but I believe in the very fiber of my being, in the absolute depth of my soul, that those of us who are privileged to live in this magnificent day and time have a sacred ministry to fulfill, including the solemn responsibility to search out that ministry and grasp it to our bosom. Let me outline just a few aspects of the spiritual life, the divine mission each of us can pursue, the call Christ gives us to "seek . . . first the kingdom of God, and his righteousness" (Matthew 6:33).

One aspect of that ministry is highlighted in this clarion call from the prophet Alma in the Book of Mormon: "This was the ministry unto which ye were called . . . to prepare [your] minds; or rather that salvation might come unto them, that [you] may prepare the minds of [your] children to hear the word at the time of [Christ's] coming" (Alma 39:16).

We need to prepare ourselves and we especially need to prepare our children to hear the word of the Lord at the time of Christ's coming. Is it possible? Is it even remotely possible that Christ cannot come because we are not prepared and have not prepared our children to receive him? Or to say that in a slightly different way, what responsibility do we have to usher in the Millennium? I don't know about you, but I would love to have the Millennium start tomorrow—or today, if that isn't sounding overly anxious. As painful as the world has become for many, and with so much evil and ill will in it, can you begin to comprehend the pain that our heavenly parents must suffer? Can you not imagine with me that Christ longs to come and bring peace, security, and tranquillity once again to this earth? I am sure he does, and I hope it is soon.

But he is bound by divine laws and heavenly circumstances, and he cannot make our home his home until we have prepared ourselves and proven ourselves worthy of his earthly company. And quite apart from our own preparation, it is the preparation of his little ones, the children that he always loved so very much—it is our role as mothers and teachers and examples to the next generation that is so crucial in this increasingly wicked world. God looks to us to bless and teach and protect the children, a generation who must hear, comprehend, understand and love his words at the time of his coming.

Listen to the urgency of the prophetic voice of President Ezra Taft Benson on this subject. Speaking to the entire Church, he said:

"This is the last and great dispensation in which the great consummation of God's purposes will be made, . . . the nucleus around which will be builded the great kingdom of God on the earth. The kingdom of heaven and the kingdom of God on the earth will be combined together at Christ's coming—and that time is not far distant. How I wish we could get the vision of this work, the genius of it, and realize the nearness of that great event. I am sure it would have a sobering effect upon us if we realized what is before us" (*Teachings of Ezra Taft Benson*, 19).

No one knows when Christ will come; not even the angels of heaven know exactly when that time is. And it doesn't matter when he comes if *we* are prepared. But many are becoming spiritually aware this is a time of hastening. The past few years have shown us that changes of everlasting consequence are evolving rapidly, in the Church and in the world around us.

Those who will open their eyes to see will recognize Christ calling them to assume their part in this ministry. I can't comprehend the degree of misery we each may feel when we stand before Christ, who paid such a price for our peace, if we cannot say to him, "I have glorified thee on the earth: I have finished the work which thou gavest me to do" (John 17:4).

That is why we can't waste much time or energy or emotion on what dress to wear or whose backyard is the biggest. We have *real* things to think about, things of the kingdom of God and the peace promised to his children. If we could spiritually pause and reflect just a little more often, we would remember that each of us has made sacred promises and covenants that we would willingly carry on our very shoulders the leadership of this people until, as He says, "I shall come in my glory with the powers of heaven" (3 Nephi 28:7).

Some days those burdens on our shoulders seem very heavy, particularly, I think, when we are concerned about our loved ones—especially the children, and what their future will be. Some days our shoulders hardly seem broad enough to face some of these tasks in the kingdom, but that is when we must remember it is *Christ's* shoulders that make the difference, that ultimately he will carry the greater load for us.

Who among us has not cried out for comfort in Christ? Even Alma, in all his righteousness, cried, "O Lord, my heart is exceedingly sorrowful; wilt thou comfort my soul in Christ." And then, because of Alma's great faith, "the Lord . . . gave them strength, that they should suffer no manner of afflictions, save it were swallowed up in the joy of Christ" (Alma 31:31, 38).

Christ's promise to us forever is that we don't have to do it alone. So let's keep our focus on the right motives, let's just try to look to him for life, let us try to lay up for ourselves treasures in heaven rather than on earth. Then we find the fulfilling of his promise, "My yoke is easy, and my burden is light." Christ has promised us in the hope of his gospel message that we "shall find rest unto [our] souls" (Matthew 11:28–30). There is no other place. There is no other way.

And I want to say this now, lest anyone misunderstand. Although life has its challenges, and our needs and those of others are great (overwhelming, it seems, at times), nevertheless the gospel of Jesus Christ is not meant to be difficult. Sometimes we as parents or leaders take something that is really very simple and make it difficult. We give it too much structure. There can be too many meetings—too much material—too many programs. These, too, are some of those "things" Christ said we shouldn't be so concerned with and consumed by. We must try hard to remember that the gospel of Jesus Christ was meant to be beautifully simple! And surely it is simply beautiful! This is, at heart, a spiritual work, a spiritual kingdom, and God will give us the spirit to succeed. It is not meant to be a merry-go-round we can't seem to get off, or an endless series of functions and frustrations that just exhaust us. Every Church meeting, every Church program, every fireside, every missionary effort, every temple endowment, every duty we perform is meant to have spiritual meaning, spiritual consequence, bringing us some portion of greater joy. So let's simplify what we can and enjoy all of it a lot more—including the yoke and burden part.

The secret, of course, is to pray earnestly that we will have enough energy just to do the truly essential things— the spiritual things, the eternal things. Then we can pray equally fervently that we will have peace regarding the nonessential things—even if some of those nonessentials seem to be Church-related too. There are many, many nonessential things to let go of if we are going to allow ourselves adequate time and freedom to embrace God. But it is worth it. For when we embrace him, he will embrace us! And to do it we must, at least in some areas of our lives, stop being too temporally focused and so telestially preoccupied.

If embracing God in this way does not yet seem easy to do, or worse yet easy to get others whom we dearly love to do, please try hard to see the task in a new way. Consider that it can be a beautifully simple and simply beautiful answer to our problems. I ask us to see ourselves as women differently than we customarily do. I ask us to see ourselves and each other as having within us that God-given spirituality and eternal focus that I believe women are born with, that women have, as the Prophet Joseph Smith said, as part of their "natures" (see *Teachings of the Prophet Joseph Smith* [Deseret Book, 1976], 226). Let's give the celestial woman within us a chance to break through all the telestial, temporal trappings we hang on her, and see what powers she might bring to these latter-day tasks if we just dig down deep inside and let her have her chance.

Listen to this call God has given to us as women: "Awake, and arise from the dust, O Jerusalem; yea, and put on thy beautiful garments, O daughter of Zion; . . . strengthen thy stakes and enlarge thy borders forever . . . that the covenants of the Eternal Father which he hath made unto thee . . . may be fulfilled" (Moroni 10:31).

The phrase "O daughter of Zion" was Moroni's metaphor for all the house of Israel, but I deeply believe it applies literally to women, especially in these last days, and specifically as it relates to our influence in our times. What are these beautiful garments spoken of? Why does the Savior use the example of women—daughters of Zion—who will strengthen our stakes, enlarge our borders, and bring everlasting joy?

Several years ago Sister Ardeth Kapp, Sister Maurine Turley, and I sat in counsel with several of the Brethren to form the Young Women values, pledge, and motto. During this consultation President Thomas S. Monson stood one day, and with all of his stature (which is very large) as a witness for Christ, he stated, "Remember, women are not to be the caboose, and they are not the engine. They are much, much more than either of these."

Since that statement I have pondered and prayed often about a woman's "divine worth." I have asked myself, What did President Monson mean by much, much more? Many years after that experience I was reading and rereading my scriptures for illuminating insight. One bright, crisp British morning in Solihull, England, as I was sequestered with my scriptures, I read this verse in the book of Revelation:

"And there appeared a great wonder in heaven; a woman clothed with the sun, and the moon under her feet, and upon her head a crown of twelve stars" (Revelation 12:1).

Now, I know that the Book of Revelation is allegorical and symbolic. There are several interpretations given to the woman in the passage I just quoted. However there must be profound purpose—again—in the Lord's selecting the symbol of a women to represent something of the glory and grandeur of God's power and influence in the last days.

As I read that scripture that morning, the sun shining brilliantly upon that written page, I can truly say that suddenly the glory and beauty and blessings of womanhood were illuminated in my heart. In my mind's eye I literally saw a woman—a woman like you—clothed with the sun, the moon under her feet, wearing a crown of stars. And the glory around from all those celestial sources was light! To my limited view I could see a woman as a transmitter, a conveyor, a conduit of light. I could see that a woman can, if she so lives for it, be the medium through which true gospel light can pass to or be conveyed from one sphere to another.

Please, please do not misunderstand me. I do not see women as having greater knowledge or wisdom than men, and this has nothing to do with priesthood, which is solely the responsibility of men to bear. What I do see is the force, even the calling, a woman has to kindle and share spirituality within her sphere of influence. I believe she has within her such a bright spiritual spark that when it is fully awakened it will ignite not only her own glory but the glory of all those to whom she is called to render service—especially her own loved ones. President James E. Faust has said it more plainly. He said that because of a woman's innate "charitable" nature, she can have (if she lives for it) a direct pipeline to God.

I believe that before we can be blessed with the Savior's presence again on this earth, the men of the priesthood will need to rise to their fully authorized power and influence, as outlined in the eighty-fourth section of the Doctrine and Covenants. I also believe that will never happen until women awaken and arise to the full potential of their adjoining and appropriate power and influence, standing faithfully with and in support of the priesthood bearers of this Church.

Satan has long known of the illuminating influence women can generate, of the power that we can promote. He knows a great deal of the glory of the sun and the moon and the stars, primarily because that could have been his inheritance and he lost it—lost all of it. It is terribly sad that the literal meaning of the name *Lucifer* is "bearer of light"— which he once was but from which privilege he fell to a kingdom of no glory and no light. Since his tragic fall from grace, I personally think his greatest ploy has been to keep us so busy with insignificant things, so mindlessly distracted from matters of real consequence, that our souls are kept from supping often with the Lord. He bids us put our light under a bushel, covering over our glory of the sun and the moon and the stars with things—materialistic and temporal and tedious.

It is a constant battle to receive and in turn provide light, truth, spiritual nourishment, and safety for God's children. That battle in and for the lives of women may be greater in our day than at any other time in the history of the world. We are all subject to dark days and flagging faith, but I have deep convictions that God has in his infinite compassion provided for us a safe place, a wilderness kingdom where he protects us against evil and nourishes us with strength. But we have to take the time to go to that wilderness retreat, we have to make the time—we have to turn a few things down and turn a few things off. We have to be prayerfully positioned in some solitude and serenity to receive the message of what is always a "still, small voice."

May I close with my most earnest effort to be reassuring. I know that much of what I have written here may seem very distant to one whose heart may be aching, or worse yet breaking, over something that is very real and very painful and very immediate. A woman illuminated by the sun and the moon and the stars, free from concerns in a telestial world, may be of little consolation if you are somewhere in the downstairs closet of despair! All of us have difficult days. All of us sometimes feel trapped by the temporary and the tedious. None of us have all we would like of heaven in a d that has quite a bit of influence from hell. I know that, and I can promise you that the prophets and apostles of the Church know it, since I have had a pretty close look at at least one of them for the last little while.

But just because we have challenges and opposition, just because sometimes it seems like it is two steps forward and one step back (or even one step forward and two steps back!), nevertheless we reach for the sun and the moon and the stars. We still keep trying to lay up for ourselves treasures in heaven and to stop worrying about all those cubits here on earth. We have faith, and we keep trying. In that spirit I leave with you just one passage of scripture, a common passage known not only to every Latter-day Saint but to almost every Christian or Jew who has owned a Bible. I speak of the comforting beauty and the eternal promises of the Twenty-third Psalm—a passage I was led to one day many years ago at a time in my life when I really needed it, and I have needed it many times since then.

Listen to these wonderfully familiar words: "The Lord is my shepherd; I shall not want." Isn't he saying, "Trust me, believe me, fix your faith in me, hand over all your fears, worries, doubts, and anxieties. I will be your shepherd, I will protect and love you, I will provide for your every need." Isn't he saying that even if there are temporary lacks in our lives, eventually we shall have all, everything? We shall want for nothing.

This scripture goes on to say, "He maketh me to lie down in green pastures." Note the verb that is used here: "He *maketh*." It sounds to me like whether we want it or not he will make us to lie down in green pastures—at least that is his desire.

This phrase has a very deep and personal meaning for me. I have witnessed so often in my life just how literally the Good Shepherd can make his sheep find comfort and peace despite some of our best efforts *not* to trust, *not* to give over, to hesitate when he beckons us to come to green pastures where our souls can be restored beside still waters.

That inclination not to trust, that tendency not to have the faith we ought to have, undoubtedly robs us of some of God's greatest blessings. I am reminded of the little dialogue:

"Come to the edge," he said.

"No, we will fall."

"Come to the edge," he said.

"No, we will fall."

"Come to the edge," he said.

So we came to the edge, he pushed us—and we flew.

This beautiful psalm continues with one marvelous promise after another. "He restoreth my soul." What an absolutely wonderful promise when our very souls have struggled and been weary! "He leadeth me in the paths of righteousness for his name's sake. Yea, though I walk through the valley of the shadow of death, I will fear no evil: for thou art with me; thy rod and thy staff they comfort me," and so on to the end of those six short verses.

Green pastures and still waters. Paths of righteousness and a cup that runneth over. Comfort and goodness and mercy all the days of our life. I simply can't imagine more encouragement or more hope than God, our Heavenly Father, gives his children—you and me and all of *our* children—his little lambs, one and all.

Once in my life I was very close to death—somewhere very deep in the valley of that shadow I have just mentioned, so deep (I learned later) that I really wasn't expected to make the journey back. Fortunately I was in a hospital at the time with very anxious doctors and nurses doing all they could for me. Out of that valley I made one desperate call— I am told it was scarcely audible but it was uttered in full faith in the Good Shepherd who had so many other times prepared a table before me and anointed my head with oil. My cry in that situation was for my husband and the priesthood I knew he bore.

It would not be appropriate to go into details here, but I wish you to know that the very moment, the absolute instant that my husband burst into that emergency room and laid his hands upon my head, I began to stabilize—my breathing returned, my heart rate ceased dropping, and eventually the other vital signs stabilized and returned to their proper functioning.

That was one dramatic example in my life, but it is not the only example—in my life or yours—in which the Lord has been our shepherd and has restored our souls. My prayer for all of us is that we will take the Lord at his word, that we will understand he means what he says: He *will* lead us in the paths of righteousness and his rod and staff *will* comfort us. I testify that the Lord *is* our shepherd, that God is our Father and Jesus Christ is his Son, and that the gospel is the only sure way for us to "fear no evil." May goodness and mercy follow us all the days of our life and may we dwell in the house of the Lord forever, I pray.

5

Goodly Parents:
Reflections of Divinity

The challenge of parenting—of becoming goodly or Godlike in our care and protection of His little ones—is surely the highest and holiest of assignments. My own goodly parents, now in their mid-eighties, still follow the struggles of each of their children, grandchildren, and great-grandchildren. We were once seven and now we have grown to more than 107. How can we thank them for their enduring, long-suffering, ever-abiding faith? I love them, and I'm grateful for their love for me. Because my parents have been reflections of divinity, I have been blessed to comprehend loving, caring, merciful heavenly parents.

Sister Jean Turley once shared with me an experience with her tiny granddaughter. She said that her granddaughter Stacy and the other little children in her Primary class were being taught a lesson on how to recognize the Savior. The children were all gathered around as the Primary teacher held up a picture of the baby Christ child in a manger scene. The teacher pointed out each person in the picture, asking the children to name them. As she came to the baby Jesus, little Stacy Turley raised her small hand, responding eagerly. "I know! I know! I know who he is! He is my brother, Jesus Turley."

What a beautifully taught child! It's wonderful that Stacy's relationship to her Savior should seem so natural and personal to her. How grateful we are for parents who have provided the strength of that teaching. At the same time it is chilling to remember that Stacy is not much younger than the little six-year-old boy who shot and killed his classmate in Michigan. What of the nurturing and teaching in his young life? We consider these two very different stories from two comparably aged children and then ask: How can we emphasize the need for irreplaceable parental guidance and nurturing in this disheveled society, before that society destroys itself?

In a recent conversation with a personal friend, a physician, I discussed some of these challenges and problems in our society. I then asked what any of us could do—leaders, teachers, public officials, and all—to strengthen the parent-child relationship. I even pressed him a little and asked him if he could, in one or two sentences, state the core of what parents should do to safeguard their children. He said simply, "With babies and young children I would say that parents should spend most of their time loving them, spending time with them. If parents are there to respond to a child's needs at these earliest stages, they will have done well in their assignment as parents."

His comments reinforced what I already knew. Looking back, I realize again that loving and lasting relationships with children begin in the earliest years of their lives. That is private, even sacred time with our children that will never come again. Being there and loving them is our specific assignment in those years when a mother is needed most, though it seems to me a mother is always needed. These are not grandma's years, or a day care's years, or years with any other caretakers, no matter how competent they may be. I believe with all of my heart that during those years our most important task is simply to be there!

Now, may I immediately say that I know how painful or even offensive that will be for some to hear. I know that in many situations there is almost literally no choice but for mothers, especially single mothers, to work. I know that in such cases other people must help fill in the gaps at home. But if this is the case, then it is the parents' urgent responsibility to spend *what time they can* with their children and to find the most nurturing of caretakers possible for that period which has to be covered some other way. We must make sure that our children are safely in the hands of people who genuinely love them. No child should be placed in a home or play school or day-care center that hasn't been inspected by physical and emotional health agents. We insist that this be done in our public restaurants. Isn't it far more important that the care and well-being of our children be protected?

Then, as soon as the challenges of life allow, bring your children home and be home with them. I say this with all the urgency I can convey. They will be grown and gone soon enough. May God bless us all, and our children, in those crucial, early developmental years at home.

One of the things you can do in these early years— indeed all of their lives—is to build your children's self-esteem. No one knows your child like you do and no one loves him or her as much as you do. Each time you feed her when she's hungry, change her diaper when it's dirty, or hug her when she cries, you are telling your daughter that you care about her and love her, and she grows up with the idea that someone is on her side, someone is helping her be happy. Where you choose to spend your time tells your son he is your treasure, he has intrinsic value, and you are his very best friend in all the world. In such ways you impress upon your children that you will be there for them in this often selfish and sometimes hostile world. Your actions are their promise that someone loves them more than they love themselves and surely more than the outside world loves them. They are secure in knowing that someone desires their peace and protection above all else in life. This remarkable kind of love and self-esteem, even before they recognize it as such, gives your children an earthly vision and deep reminder of the relationships they had with parents in heaven.

That early self-esteem can sustain a child all his or her life. My close friend Julie Pederson is a young professional woman, not yet married. She, like all the rest of us, struggles from time to time with fears about her future and its opportunities—or lack of them. Sometimes those feelings can tug at her self-esteem. She told me that on those occasional blue days when she looks in the mirror and doesn't see what she would like to see, it is hard to feel good about herself. At such times she feels awkward and confused and uncomforted. But she says she has learned in those "hopeless but tender moments" to try very hard to remember the love and joy she saw in her mother's eyes when her mother looked at her as a child. Looking back at how her mother adored her helps her know again that she is deeply valued, inherently beautiful, and a woman of limitless possibilities.

That experience with Julie reminded me of something my own daughter-in-law Jeanne once said to me. Jeanne was an excellent student all through school. As many children do, she worked her heart out for good grades—and got them. But when I asked what she loved about her home and her childhood, she got tears in her eyes and said simply, "I knew at home I wouldn't be graded. I already had my parents' love and acceptance." What a blessing! What a treasure for a child to carry! In a sense Julie and Jeanne's stories are identical. We can give such gifts to our children—gifts they will draw upon all their lives.

I want you to know that I *loved* being a mother. Aside from the love I have for my husband, I loved mothering more than anything else in the world, especially because I was told early in our marriage that I wouldn't be able to have children. So when our children came, I treasured *every* moment. I used to resent anything that intruded on that opportunity, though some things inevitably do. However, even with all the joy it brought, I learned that being an always present, always loving mother is the most demanding, fatiguing, and draining obligation that was ever placed upon my shoulders. Mothering, I believe, requires engaging every muscle, every nerve, every fiber of our being, and through it all we pray.

Let me stress what our faith can do as we address our children's needs and try to also meet some of our own. When we were born, we were all perfectly loving and lovable. Out most urgent needs at birth were to be loved, calmed, and nurtured, just as we surely were by heavenly parents before we came here. In our earliest moments we were awestruck, astonished, full of wonder. We were filled with love and had every confidence in God's continued goodness.

What happened? At what age did we begin to feel anxious, fearful, doubtful of that goodness and that sense of the miraculous?

Marianne Williamson has written that it happens "because we [are eventually] taught to focus elsewhere. We are taught a very negative view of the world that contradicts who we really are. We are taught to think thoughts like competition, struggle, sickness, finite resources, limitation, guilt, and pride—as a result we begin to know these first-hand. We are taught that things like earning grades, being good enough, having money, and doing things the proper way, are more important than love, trust and confidence. We are taught that we're separate from other people, that we have to compete to get ahead, that we're not quite good enough the way we are. We are taught to see the world the way that others have come to see it. The thinking of the world began pounding in our ears almost the moment we hit shore. Love is what we were born with. Fear is what we have learned here" (*A Return to Love* [Harper Collins, 1996], n.p.).

What have we lost, and where did faith go? Are our

lives as individuals, as children, and eventually as parents fragmented with the fears and feelings of the natural man? Are our minds and hearts filled with unkind thoughts, jealousy, and anger? Are we simply too uptight about too many things too much of the time? Do we negatively compare our children with other children or our material circumstances with those of other parents? Are we just too inclined to self-doubt, worry, anxiety, and fear?

If we answer "yes" to the above—and we all do at least some of the time—then we need to grab our thinking by the lapels and shake it up a bit. In a word, we need to repent. We need to have faith. We are not our grades or our talents, our money, our jobs, or even our Church callings. We are more than that. We are potential gods and goddesses, and so are our children. In Abraham 4:27 we are told that we were formed "in the image of the Gods."

If we don't love ourselves and our children enough to see in them and in ourselves God's image, what in our thinking needs to be changed or relinquished or unlearned? What do we have to let go of in order to see with these newer eyes of pure revelation? What we have to let go of are Satan's lies—the negative thoughts that he has planted and that we have too often allowed to grow.

I testify that God loves us completely, that we are his spirit children, and in that regard we are literally brothers and sisters with Christ, as little Stacy Turley so intuitively understood. God did not form any of us to be higher or lower than another. He is our Father, and we all have eternal access to his love, his peace, his miracles, his joy, and every other blessing he has in store for those who love him. But sometimes he will let us struggle on the way to those blessings.

Forgive me if I insert here an experience from my own family. Our two-and-a-half-year-old grandson, Jake, is a robust little boy, "an accident waiting to happen," as his father often describes him. Just recently he ran into the corner of the kitchen table and cut his head pretty sharply right above the eye. As expected with most head wounds, he was bleeding profusely.

Our daughter-in-law Paige was home with Jake and his seven-month-old sister but no daddy nearby to help. So she drove bleeding son and amazed baby daughter to the emergency room of the hospital, managing all this as best she could.

What follows is Paige's own account of this incident:

"We had about a two-hour wait, during which I got more and more nervous. I was worrying about my baby being sick and hungry. I was worrying about my sweet little Jakey having to be strapped in a body-length restraining jacket and going through the terribly painful process of having stitches. I wondered if Matt would get any of the messages I'd left with people on campus. I started worrying about medical bills, scarring, and trying to keep sunscreen on a fresh wound. I could feel tears welling up in my eyes.

"Shortly after this, Matt walked in the door, and we were finally called in to meet with the doctor. Relieved to see my husband and strengthened by a scripture I had just read, I took great hope. But the Lord was not yet finished teaching me about this important principle.

"As Jake was being prepared to get his stitches, he was alarmed and scared. When the nurses strapped him into the restraining jacket that tied him down from his shoulders to his feet, he became even more alarmed. However, it was when they put a sanitized cloth over his face so he could not see the doctor coming at him with a big needle that Jake got absolutely terrified and hysterical. At the top of his lungs, in a cry I was sure could be heard around the entire hospital, he screamed, 'I can't see you, Daddy, I can't see you, Daddy.'

"It was amazing to me that of all the frightening things that were happening to him, not being able to see his daddy was the most terrifying of all. So, with the doctor's help, we arranged the cloth so that Jake could not see what the doctor was doing but could still see his daddy.

"In reflecting on this afterwards, I thought how true this is of our earthly lives. Nothing could be more terrifying than not having our focus on our Heavenly Father. Here we too must make whatever arrangements are necessary to keep our eyes on God as we are assailed by the pains, temptations, and trials of life. It will keep our hope alive and give us strength.

"The other thing that was revealed to me in this brief but rather traumatic moment was a glimpse of what it must be like for God to watch us, his children, go through our struggles here on earth. As the doctor started stitching and I stood there listening to my precious little boy, flesh of my flesh and bone of my bone, cry out for me to hold him and make the doctor go away, I felt emotions as deep as any I've ever experienced.

"With all of my heart I wanted to go to him, knock Matt and the doctor out of the way, tear off the restraining jacket and grab Jake, hold him in my arms, and tell him everything was going to be okay. But I didn't. As much as I wanted to, I couldn't because I knew that what he was going through was best for him. If I had stepped in to prevent the painful process to clean and close that wound, he would have been left, for the rest of his life, with a large, visible scar. Or worse, the wound could have gotten infected and become an even greater problem, causing even more pain.

"So *because* I loved him, I did *not* run to him to rescue him from his momentary agony. Instead I stood there and allowed Jacob to suffer for a moment. But I did not stand far away. I was right there by his side, suffering with him and calling out to him that everything would soon be all right. He often could not hear me because he was crying so loudly, or see me because his vision was blocked, but I was there at every second, watching the doctor's work like a hawk and comforting Jakey as best I could. And at that time, nothing in the entire world, not wild horses or threat of physical harm could have made me leave my suffering child. I was with him, and I was not moving."

Then she concludes, "If that is what I was feeling at that moment for my Jakey, I can only imagine how much closer and more immovably a God of perfect love and goodness must stand by any of us when we, his children, are crying out wondering why we have to go through what we are going through, why it has to hurt so much, and why the pain does not seem to stop. It is hard for me to imagine that God loves us more than I love Jacob, or Mitzi, or Matthew, but I know that he does. And because of that love, and his matchless power, I know we can have perfect hope in him."

If our souls will not be stilled by these verities and truths, how can we possibly hope to teach them to our children? If we feel ourselves wavering in these matters, let us determine together that we will here and now begin a long spiritual journey inward, that we will plumb the depths of our own souls until we remember and seal into our minds forever that God's gifts are those of a perfect parent, that he loves us with a love that will never falter or fail. Remember: "Love is what we were born with. Fear is what we have learned here."

One advantage we have in pursuing these feelings successfully is that our minds have been preset with celestial dials and directions. Those preearthly tendencies can be remembered with peaceful, trusting prayers and quiet, thoughtful meditation. Through prayer and supplication, we can have God again reveal to us our true worth and beauty.  The truth of who we really are can be revealed day by day even as Christ's atonement renews our soul week by week at the sacrament table. Our mistakes and fears can melt into the pure water we drink and the purity of the bread we eat as we partake of it and echo the sacramental prayers with our own supplications. And all this we can teach to our children.

While we are in the process of doing this, of finding strength for our parenting task, let us remember we are as perfect as a budding rose whose petals are still unfolding one by one until our divine identity completes its flower and fruition. We may at times have chosen a wrong behavior or made a miscalculation as a parent, but our divine nature is still perfect, and so is the source of our divine help. As we actively repent and forgive ourselves we become whole *and* holy. This process of spiritual restoration presents a practical path for our little ones to follow. Children are able to learn and renew as they privately view *our* growth and experience. No greater gift could be given to a child than the gift of renewal through faith and repentance, leading to the gift of renewal through the ordinances and the gift of the Holy Spirit.

Above all else, we need to give our children the gospel. I don't think it is too strong to suggest that we are, in a poet's phrase, "small gods" to our children. They watch us and find hope. Furthermore, I believe that when we see the divine in ourselves and in all else that God has created, we will see the divine in our children, even one who for a time might seem unwilling to be divine. Let us remember that they are "small gods" as well.

I heard recently of a little boy who was having an argument with his father. The father had set some limits for the child but had used some rather harsh words in doing so. The little boy responded, "You can't treat me like that."

"Why not?" asked the father.

"Because my Heavenly Father didn't treat me that way."

"And how do you know better than I do how our Heavenly Father acts?" said the father.

The little boy answered, "Because I saw him last."

Our children have most recently been with their heavenly parents. We should not be surprised if they remember much more than we do. Perhaps they still remember the gospel in a more complete fulness than we do. Perhaps that is why they can't speak for a time. I testify that children know instinctively how people should act. And even when they can't verbally tell us exactly what they know and feel, if we are sensitive and in tune with their hearts, they find a way of letting us know, even the tiny ones. Their unsullied, unhampered souls are still so sensitive, so true, and so trusting. If we neglect or mistreat them, or if our actions do not match up to what they know we believe to be true, it is as though they see these acts through a magnifying glass. Any action unworthy of a parent seems to be enlarged tenfold. A truly serious transgression can plow a furrow so deeply into their little brains that their view of right and wrong can be troubled for a very long time.

Of the many things that a child can learn positively from a parent, think how glorious it would be for a child to learn how *not* to pass on a misfortune or a misperception received from an earlier generation. Think how glorious it would be if they could see a forgiving attitude, hear us speak well of other virtues, watch us look in all such matters toward the Savior, the only source that can heal and set things right again.

My husband's father, Frank Holland, was left fatherless at three months of age. His widowed mother remarried when Frank was about ten years old. Even at an early age, Frank loved books and learning above any other activity. His new stepfather, however, was a man who had suffered disabilities in World War I that impaired him physically and damaged him emotionally. He not only took out his anger on his wife and his two boys but also took the boys out of school. In Frank's case that was in the seventh grade, and that hurt him more deeply even than the physical or verbal abuse he received. Home life for my future father-in-law was anything but heavenly before that family found the restored gospel. It was more like something out of Charles Dickens's *Oliver Twist*.

Late in his life, when my father-in-law suffered a heart attack and lay dying in the hospital, I had the privilege to assist my angel mother-in-law in attending to his needs. The most painful moment of that whole painful experience was to see him once in a somewhat delirious state, curled up in a near-fetal position, pleading, "Daddy, please don't hit me."

We all know the psychological theory that abusive parents inevitably beget abusive children. That may be a general truism, but I testify that it isn't—and doesn't need to be a universal truth, because my beloved father in law stopped that cycle in his generation. My husband watched his father struggle with a sense of inadequacy and sorrow that was heart-wrenching at times. However, Jeff also watched his father fight against those adversities with conversion to the gospel, love of Latter-day Saint life, and especially love of the Book of Mormon. He watched his father love people, particularly his own children, in spite of the kind of childhood he himself had experienced. He saw him pore over his scriptures and pray to see his Heavenly Father not as one who is punishing and judgmental but as one who loves us perfectly even with all of our flaws and imperfections, and, yes, even when some mistakes have been made by earlier generations of parents, if that happened. I think it is safe to say that no father ever loved his children more or was kinder to them in every way than Frank Holland was to his. That is a parenting miracle very close to my life, so I feel duty-bound to acknowledge such heaven-sent power, such divine ability to change in one generation what must be changed for the children's—and the gospel's—sake.

I pay tribute to that wonderful father-in-law whom I loved as much as he loved me, and to all the other parents of the world who have risen above difficulties to make life better for their children than they had it themselves. Jeff's father broke the chain. In light of my husband's present service, it is inspiring to note that his father was instrumental in teaching him something of a deeper meaning regarding turning the hearts of the children to the fathers, and the hearts of the fathers to the children (see D&C 2). That turning now includes the hearts of my children and my grandchildren and all of our posterity that will yet come down through all of time. As parents and as children, we do not need to be captive to patterns of destructive behavior or to schools of psychological thought. We can know and love and exercise the truth, and the truth can set us free (see John 8:32).

We learn again and again that this relationship between parent and child is welded and sealed with one quality— love. Love alone is the path to everything else, including patience, forgiveness, and restoring what might have been lost. When we decide to love, everyone within our sphere of influence has a chance to triumph. And we can decide to love because through it all God first loved us (see 1 John 4:19).

In order for us to acquire these gospel virtues and help our children acquire them, we must give ourselves to the Lord, as Paul counseled the Romans: "Present your bodies a living sacrifice, holy, acceptable unto God, which is your reasonable service. And be not conformed to this world: but be ye transformed by the renewing of your mind, that ye may prove what is that good, and acceptable, and perfect, will of God" (Romans 12:1–2).

I love Paul for freely admitting his earlier mistakes in life. If he can say we are, after repentance, acceptable unto God, I believe him! I also believe that if we offered with Paul this same prayer, God would keep us from "conforming to the world." Surely the Lord will, if invited, renew our minds and, where necessary, change our directions. We can then be transformed into the power of our own divine possibilities.

This is how we teach! This is how we prove to our children what it is that is good, what is "acceptable and the perfect will of God." God can perform miracles, and with him we can become master over our parental challenges.  Miracles can flow forever and forever to our children, our grandchildren, and our great-grandchildren. There is no space in our minds for doubt or fear where God is privileged to reign.

None of this is meant to diminish the seriousness of the real problems and the heartache some parents face. That physician friend I mentioned earlier said something about this. He said, "There are parents with older children, especially teenagers, who are experiencing paroxysms of pain because their child doesn't seem to be turning out well. In trying to assuage their broken hearts I continually remind each of them, 'It wasn't your assignment to live your children's life for them. Your assignment was to nurture and love them to the best of your ability, teaching and informing them clearly about choices and their consequences.' In the end, after we have done all we can do, it is the child who will determine how well he or she turns out by the choices he or she will make. Moral agency is, alas, still a fact of family life."

I have seen some teenagers whose choices in life would seem to have severed forever their relationship not only to their parents but to God himself. Some have made choices so perverse that it would seem even the angels of heaven would be taxed in trying to provide a remedy. Yet I have seen their parents choose long-suffering and patience that would rival Job's, and because of their continual praying with all energy of heart for that particular child, their relationship over time—sometimes over decades, sometimes over an entire lifetime—has been restored. It has taken "a living sacrifice," to use Paul's phrase, but the blessings *have* come.

Whenever I was hurting as a small child, I would go to my parents. Their first words of comfort were, "Yes, we understand the problem. Have you talked to your Heavenly Father about this?" As a teenager, with all the complexities and ups and downs of those years, I would go to my parents, and though I would insist my problems were unique in all the world and absolutely beyond help (all teenage problems are unique and beyond help), they would say, "Yes, we know, but there is God." Even now, I go to them when pressures mount and the demands of life seem overwhelming.

By the faith and continual counsel of my parents I have come to that child's knowledge that there is a Father (and a Mother) in Heaven whose relationship with me is all powerful, all encompassing, and as close to me in a divine way as my earthy parents' relationship is with me in mortality. Now, watching my parents endure the onset of age and the adversity of declining health, I echo back to them that God loves them and that he is always there. They deserve to have confidence return if and when their childlike anxieties surface again as age increases. We should *never* fear. When we are old, our children can calm us even as we calmed them.

Because of all this—the goodliness of my own parents and my husband's parents, the heritage that has been given to my children and my grandchildren—I can declare that home is where I long to be. I want to be there, fixed and sure, when I am needed in any generation. I also know that when my family members, young and old, come to me in their struggles, they need to see me at my best. I want them to touch a hand that is calm, one that is undergirded with confidence, one that conveys strength and compassion and, if it is ever necessary, forgiveness. I want them to see charity in my eyes and feel the Spirit of the Holy Ghost in my home. I want them to know I am their mother, their grandmother, their sister, their daughter. I want with all my heart to reflect the love and strength of heaven as I join hands with God in protecting and blessing the souls of the children he has been good enough to send to and through me.

No work in this world is sweeter or more holy than parenting, and no security should be greater than that which a child feels at home. I believe it to be at the heart of "the good and acceptable and perfect will of God." I know he will help us succeed in this, his true work.

6

A Meek and Quiet Spirit

Twenty-two years ago I lost a baby that I had carried through the sixth month of pregnancy. This was a long-awaited baby for whom my husband, three young children, and I had prayed earnestly.

I felt deeply bereft. I struggled with after-baby blues—but without a baby to compensate—and endured aching, empty arms. Then my doctors confirmed that the complications surrounding the loss of the baby would preclude my chances of having any more children. My already broken heart now felt completely shattered.

While I was struggling to come to grips with this loss, and at the same time trying to comfort Jeff and my children, who were also sorrowing, an unanticipated professional assignment was given to my husband. This singular opportunity, with the financing of most of our meager savings, took all five of us to the Holy Land. We were thrilled to have two weeks together in Jerusalem at Christmastime.

When we arrived, my husband attended the meetings to which he had been assigned while I took the beautiful children I *did* have and visited the sacred scenes of the Old and New Testaments. One evening, exhausted after a long day of sightseeing with the children and still struggling with my emotions, I quickly tucked my children in for the night. My husband was away at another meeting. I had the whole evening to myself.

As I stood at the window of our hotel room overlooking the Holy City, instead of being grateful for such an opportunity and for the blessings I did have in such great abundance, I suddenly felt very, very sorry for myself. Then, to  add another blow, I recognized that self-pity and immediately felt guilty for not being able to just snap out of it. (Sometimes we can be so hard on ourselves!) At that age I hadn't yet learned that the perfectly understandable fatigue that can come to a young mother can put her into a dull, gray world where for a time it seems impossible to find the bright light of day.

I stood there for a long time, thinking it was difficult to be a woman. I had just that day visited the tombs of Sarah, Rebecca, and Rachel, and at that moment in time all I could see were their sacrifices, hardships, and the disappointments they had encountered.

I wondered about the children they had lost or couldn't bear. I wondered about their heavy hearts and challenging lives. How did they endure what they endured in far more difficult times than my own? I started to weep in my silent grief and felt so terribly alone in it.

In the midst of the tears I offered a little prayer, asking as honestly as I knew how for heavenly light and information. Literally just seconds into my prayer, I felt the promptings of the Holy Spirit telling me to open my scriptures. I concluded my prayer and opened my Bible. The passage I first saw was 1 Peter 3:6, where my eyes fell upon the name *Sara* and the words, "whose daughters ye are, as long as ye do well, and are not afraid with any amazement."

Well, I was not afraid but I certainly was amazed that I would turn at random to a passage of scripture so relevant to my personal circumstances. The Lord definitely had my attention, but without having had much experience in this sort of thing I wondered if this was just coincidence. I was yet to learn in my life how often and how dramatically the Lord would speak directly to me through the Spirit and especially through the scriptures.

I then read the whole third chapter of 1 Peter, which begins:

"Likewise, ye wives, be in subjection to your own husbands; that, if any obey not the word, they also may without the word be won by the conversation of the wives."

And then verses three and four:

"Whose adorning let it not be that outward adorning of

plaiting the hair, and of wearing of gold, or of putting on of apparel; But let it be the *hidden man of the heart*, in that which is not corruptible, even the ornament of a meek and quiet spirit, which is in the sight of God of great price" (1 Peter 3:1, 3–4; emphasis added).

At first I was a little offended with the word *subjection*. I knew that Paul had firm views on the role of women, but this was Peter, the chief apostle, the president of the church! My husband and I had recently left the environment of an Ivy League university where we heard daily the views of Betty Friedan, Gloria Steinem, and other striking, usually strident, articulate voices for women's rights and "liberations." In that setting I had vigorously defended my role as a stay-at-home mom and felt blessed in doing so. But now I had lost a baby, and I was blue.

The initial feelings that stirred in me when I read that first line of verse one almost caused me to stop, but I felt compelled to read on. I am so grateful that I did. I felt enormous peace wash over me with verses three and four. I knew they were the words of a loving Father in heaven through his prophet. They quickened me and lifted my heavy spirit. I can't fully explain what happened at that moment—the verses I read were nice but not that unusual—yet quite unexpectedly an unusual arousal of strength lifted me out of my lethargy and my despair. I began to feel a little of the power of that will which my father had told me character-ized my nature even in my youth. I prayed again, with even a greater sense of urgency, and meditated after I was through. In that hour I began a search for what the Lord had called "the hidden man [or woman] of the heart, [even] that which was not corruptible, even the ornament of a meek and a quiet spirit." For the first time in my life I saw "subjection" as a virtue, a synonym for "meekness" and "a quiet spirit." I felt subjection—first to God and then to oth-ers, including my husband—to be astonishingly liberating and central to the grandeur of Sarah, Rebecca, and Rachel. It was a moment of true revelation, an epiphany in the land of God's greatest epiphany.

Fast forward nearly a quarter of a century. I am now nearly sixty years old and can honestly say that I have sin-cerely studied, pondered, experimented, practiced, tried, failed, and started all over again to be meek, to have a peaceful spirit, to have a quiet heart.

I have learned that with every covenant the Lord asks of us, he showers profusely his most glorious blessings upon us, beautiful gifts too precious and sometimes even too sacred to describe. Sara and her daughters had it right— peace is in the realm of the Spirit, not in the temporal world. Bowing the head. Bending the knee. Weeping. Blessings multiplied, pressed down, and overflowing.

It is obvious that Satan will do everything in his power to see that we don't yield, that we don't give ground. He didn't, and he is determined that we won't. This devious and fallen son has successfully taken gospel principles, including the language used to describe them, and has so distorted them that many of us, both men and women, bristle when we should be bowing.

Do you think that by his description of "a quiet spirit" the Lord meant us to be mute or ignorant, social doormats? Of course not. He meant that we would be intelligent enough to put our souls at rest, that we would have an inner calm, our minds and hearts in a peaceful state. "A quiet spirit" means we are integrated, settled, stabilized, stilled from the confusing, competitive stirrings within our own egos from the ill-conceived, disappointing, and betraying incentives outside us in the world of getting gain.

If we choose to recognize only the negative aspects of such words as *submit, subject,* and *obey,* it is little wonder that women recoil at their mere mention. But if we look up the word *submission* in any good thesaurus, we will see the synonyms *patient, humble, softness, lamb-like-ness.* These words fairly shout the discipleship of Christ!

Surely that is why the ornament of a "meek and quiet spirit," in the hidden man and woman of the heart, is in the sight of God "of great price." It is of great price because it is so uncommonly rare! True disciples always are. And women have a special invitation to demonstrate these virtues and claim their special blessings.

There are glorious powers and privileges that come with keeping this covenant—gifts given by a generous God who encourages godliness in us. The Prophet Joseph Smith said of women, "If you live up to your privileges, the angels cannot be restrained from being your associates. Females, if they are pure and innocent, can come in the presence of God" (*Teachings of the Prophet Joseph Smith* [Deseret Book, 1976], 226).

And men are given the same counsel. If they are to honor the holy priesthood, they too must submit themselves, subject themselves, and bow down. "No power or influence can or ought to be maintained . . . only by persuasion, by long-suffering, by gentleness and meekness, and by love unfeigned" (D&C 121:41). That's just the way it has to be for disciples of Christ, male and female.

As I speak of our covenants to follow the counsel of a righteous man, may I quote Joseph Smith again. "Sisters always . . . concentrate [your] faith and prayers for, and place confidence in [your] husbands, whom God has appointed for [you] to honor, and in those faithful men whom God has placed at the head of the Church to lead His people, that we should arm and sustain them with our prayers" (*Teachings of the Prophet Joseph Smith*, 226).

And again from Peter: "Likewise, ye husbands, dwell with them according to knowledge [that is, the proper use of the power of the priesthood], . . . as being heirs together of the grace of life; that your prayers be not hindered" (1 Peter 3:7). Is there a more powerful or needed promise than the promise that our prayers will not be hindered? Wouldn't that entitle all of us, men and women, to receive "revelation upon revelation, knowledge upon knowledge, that thou mayest know the mysteries and peaceable things—that which bringeth joy, that which bringeth life eternal" (D&C 42:61).

Would not a person of any wisdom be willing to go and sell all that he or she has to receive such promises "of great price"? We have only to live up to our privileges to claim them. If we as daughters of Zion lived up to our possibilities, might not the kingdom of heaven be hastened in its coming? I wonder. If we lived this way for the sake of our children, might those children be the ones to prepare the earth for the return of the Savior? I wonder if the Lord is waiting for his governing principles to be lived and fully appreciated before he can reign personally upon the earth. He *will* reign, and we *will* be his subjects. We will bow down then, so perhaps it is a good idea for us to practice bowing now.

It isn't that we haven't been taught this priestly relationship for men and women. However, I think that Satan has successfully sabotaged the beauty and blessings of living it. Our egos have too willingly participated in the world's view of what it means to become "only" a husband or "only" a wife. Paul, an apostle, is often vilified for his view of women when in fact it seems to me he was only trying to elevate *both* men and women to a holier realm.

"This is a great mystery: but I speak concerning Christ and the church. Nevertheless let every one of you in particular so love his wife even as himself; and the wife see that she reverence her husband" (Ephesians 5:32–33). Christlike love from someone. Reverence in return. Sounds wonderfully sacred, even deified, to me. No loss anticipated there that I can see.

The older I become, the more I see that marriage is not a contest of wills but an orderly way to have a profound relationship. It is learning how to support each other in being the highest and holiest we can become. It is learning the true meaning and beauty and glory behind the word *submission* for *both* men and women. It is learning how to fit together in the larger body of Christ. "For we are members of his body, of his flesh, and of his bones. For this cause shall a man leave his father and mother, and shall be joined unto his wife, and they two shall be *one flesh*" (Ephesians 5:30–31; emphasis added).

Figuratively speaking, the holiest, most spiritual center

of our body is the heart. Our future has everything to do with what we desire in our hearts.

I sadly have come to understand that the greatest obstruction to my own heart and the greatest obstacle to doing God's will is my own will. We are always going to be tempted—Satan used this tactic on Christ—to put ourselves first, to be number one, to get glory, to be justified, to be sure we never play the fool, to get everything this world has to offer. It takes constant vigilance, constant evaluation of our values and our personal needs to let go of such self-centeredness and live by the heart. It takes years of practice, years of prayer, meditation, and daily scripture dedication to rid ourselves of vanity's constant demands. But it is the only path to true peace, true happiness, and a constant relationship with the Lord. That is why he softly bids, "Come unto me, . . . for I am meek and lowly in *heart,* and ye shall find rest unto your souls" (Matthew 11:28–29; emphasis added).

In other words, what Christ is saying to me is, "Don't attach yourself to images and possessions and the 'plaited hair' of the world, lest they begin to mean more to you than I do, or my Father does. Let go of your ego's need for the honors that man can bestow, and I will make myself known unto you." Enjoying that presence of the Lord is our only true and lasting joy, in time and in eternity. Everything else pales by comparison. I testify of this truth with every fiber of my being. I testify of the beauty and joy the Spirit of the Lord brings. I stand as a witness to these words of clear doctrine, as contained in the Book of Mormon:

"And now, my brethren [and sisters], I would that ye should humble yourselves before God, and bring forth fruit meet for repentance, that ye may also enter into that rest.

"Yea, humble yourselves even as the people in the days of Melchizedek, who was also a high priest after this same order which I have spoken, who also took upon him the high priesthood forever. . . .

"Now these ordinances were given after this manner, that thereby the people might look forward on the Son of God, it being a type of his order, or it being his order, and this that they might look forward to him for a remission of their sins, that they might enter into the rest of the Lord" (Alma 13:13–16).

To enter into the rest of the Lord means to enter into his full presence. I believe that before we can enter into his presence, we have to be like him, to enjoy his order, his traits, his characteristics and his form of government. To become like him, we have to desire more than every other desire to offer him our hearts and receive his in return.

"For behold, angels are declaring it unto many at this time in our land; and this is for the purpose of preparing the *hearts* of the children of men to receive his word at the time of his coming. . . . For the time cometh, we know not how soon. . . .

"And now, my brethren [and sisters], I wish from the inmost part of my *heart*, yea, with great anxiety even unto pain, that ye would hearken unto my words, and cast off your sins, and not procrastinate the day of your repentance;

"But that ye would humble yourselves before the Lord, and call on his holy name, and watch and pray continually, that ye may not be tempted above that which ye can bear, and thus be led by the Holy Spirit, becoming humble, meek, submissive, patient, full of love and all long-suffering;

"Having faith on the Lord; having a hope that ye shall receive eternal life; having the love of God always in your *hearts*, that ye may be lifted up at the last day and enter into his rest" (Alma 13:24–29; emphasis added).

Thank you, Sarah, Rebecca, and Rachel. Thank you, Peter, Paul, and Joseph Smith. Thank you, women *and* men, husbands included, to whom and with whom it is a joy to be submissive. Thank you, Lord, for bringing us into subjection and for exalting a meek and quiet spirit which is to thee of such great price.

7

God's Covenant of Peace

This is the voice of Helaman to his sons Nephi and Lehi: "Remember, remember that it is upon the rock of our Redeemer, who is Christ, the Son of God, that ye must build your foundation; that when the devil shall send forth his mighty winds, yea, his shafts in the whirlwind, yea, when all his hail and his mighty storm shall beat upon you, it shall have no power over you to drag you down to the gulf of misery and endless wo, because of the rock upon which ye are built" (Helaman 5:12).

That is the same message the Psalmist gave in another time but for the same purpose—to calm our fears and soothe our hearts, to give us refuge from the storm. Speaking of those who are caught in the rising wind and the perilous waves of life, Psalm 107:26–30 reads:

"They mount up to the heaven, they go down again to the depths: their soul is melted because of trouble. They reel to and fro, and stagger like a drunken man, and are at their wits' end. Then they cry unto the Lord in their trouble, and he bringeth them out of their distresses. He maketh the

storm a calm, so that the waves thereof are still. Then are they glad because they be quiet; so he bringeth them unto their desired haven."

On some long days and during some even longer nights you may have wondered why that comfort, that care, and that guidance are not a little more evident—or at least evident a little sooner. That reminds me of a thought expressed by Mother Teresa of Calcutta. "I was consoling a little girl who was sick and had much pain," said Teresa. "I told her, 'You should be happy that God sends you suffering, because your sufferings are a proof that God loves you much. Your sufferings are kisses from Jesus.' 'Then Mother,' answered the little girl, 'please ask Jesus not to kiss me quite so much'" (in Edward Le Joly, *Mother Teresa of Calcutta: A Biography* [Harper & Row, 1985], 321).

We will all have the chance to face some of these storm-filled, tempestuous moments in life—moments when, for a time, we feel utterly alone and experience genuine despair. Nevertheless, whatever challenges you have faced and may be facing yet, I *know* that God is caring for you, guiding you, and bringing you to his "haven." I know that partly because I know you, but I know it best of all because I know him.

I think the beginning of a new millennium is a good time for us to spiritually inventory the many changes, choices, and challenges we face individually and collectively. This is a good time to ask ourselves if we are truly built upon the rock of our Redeemer, that sure foundation upon which, if we build, we cannot fall. This is a good time to ask whether we are living in such a way that God can bring us into his "desired haven."

The most obvious external symbol of such refuge, of such safety, is the holy temple. Are we true to the covenants we have made there? Is our faith in God and in his promises such that when we enter his holy house it truly can be a sanctuary from the storm? And when we cannot be in a temple, do we keep our covenants in that other holy place, our own home, the other great sanctuary God has given to the faithful? Because of covenants made and kept, we have the blessing of taking our sanctuaries with us, much like the children of Israel did as they wound their way toward the promised land. And given the storms that can come up in the Sinais of our life, it is a wonderful thing that God goes with us.

I assume you won't think me too bold or off-base if I say that when the winds blow and the sea is storm tossed, we must not give in to self-pity. God is with us, Christ is our sure foundation, there is a safe haven ahead. We simply have to remember that in this mortal journey all learning, all personal growth, all spiritual refinement carry with them the possibility of a little motion sickness. No one—not even the Saints, maybe *especially* not the Saints—is immune from such challenges. Remember the little girl and the kisses from Jesus. No one escapes God's refining hand. Our trials offer a training ground for godhood. Without some moments in darkness, would we ever cherish the light? Without confronting some doubt, would we ever recognize and cling to faith?

I would dare say, there is not a woman in this Church who has not been directly affected by any number of things: disease or death, loneliness or discouragement, divorce or family or financial challenges—any of a wide variety of disappointments or seemingly unyielding tribulations.

Many of these challenges have come not from personal choice but from God's divine timetable, a timetable that for obvious reasons is usually *not* put into our hands for prior review and approval. The loss of a spouse, concern for a child, a major change in health or temporal circumstance—these can occur to any one of us at any time. So many things can unexpectedly play havoc with our hope and darken our view of the future.

And if these burdens do not fall upon us directly, they can come to those we love. In either case, it is no less painful to us. In fact, as a doctor friend of mine once said, "It's like asking a mother not to breathe" when she has to be only a bystander near her children who are afflicted with one kind of trial or another, feeling there is so little she can do to help. In that category some have seen their own children or grandchildren make choices so inconsistent with their own that their lives have been changed forever. At least that is how it seems in the heat and pain of the moment.

With all of this ebbing and flowing of emotion that the Psalmist described, we can, as one writer put it, "go from heaven to hell and from hell to heaven a dozen times a day" (May Sarton, *Journal of a Solitude* [W. W. Norton, 1973], 108). And on some days, particularly difficult days, it may appear that the spiral downward is more frequent than the reach upward. There are days when the adversary seems to have an absolutely crushing upper hand.

You may relate to the following passage contained in a letter from John Winthrop to his wife, Margaret. This particular letter was written in response to a situation in which their wildest and most irresponsible son married a young woman against their wishes. John Winthrop, who discovered the news while on business in London, wrote to his wife back in New England, asking her to take in their son and his new wife until they could get the means to settle on their own. Then he gave her courage with these words:

"I know thou lookest for troubles here [meaning life here on earth] and when one affliction is over, to meet with another. But remember what our Savior tells us; Be of good comfort, I have overcome the world. See his goodness, he hath conquered our enemies before hand, and by Faith in him, we shall assuredly prevail over them all. Therefore my sweet wife, raise up thy heart, and be not dismayed at the crosses thou meetest with in family affairs, or otherwise, but still fly to him, who will take up thy burden for thee, go thou on cheerfully in obedience to his holy will, in the course he hath set thee, peace shall come, thou shalt rest as in thy bed and in the mean time he will not fail nor forsake thee" (*Winthrop Papers*, 6 vols. [Massachussetts Historical Society, 1929–1947], 2:84).

I don't pretend to have any prepackaged solutions to individual sorrows, but I do know some very basic things to be true. No matter how terrible the current challenge may seem, if, as Mr. Winthrop said, we can go on cheerfully in obedience to God's holy will, peace shall come, we shall "rest in our beds," and God will not fail nor forsake us. God can mend our broken hearts. Indeed, I believe it is through the cracks of a broken heart that God sheds his purest and most illuminating light to the soul.

Please trust lovingly in the goodness of God. He will honor the covenants you have made with him! Glorious and glimmering promises await you if you will but trust in him. You are God's child. He loves you—and he will never stop loving you. You are still being formed and transformed at his tender hand. Though his molding may require that you walk through the valley of the shadow of death, he has provided for you a pathway of peace. Even through the darkest of shadows we can walk in comfort and consolation if we lovingly trust God. Remember your baptism. Remember the sacramental table. Remember the temple. Remember an entire theology built upon covenants. Well did Pierre Teilhard de Chardin write, "Not everything is immediately good to those who seek God; but everything is capable of becoming good" (*The Divine Milieu* [Harper & Row, 1960], 86). Things are *made* good through the power of covenants.

I don't know exactly how old I was, maybe fourteen or fifteen years of age, when I learned this truth. I only remember being old enough to think I had made too many mistakes in my life to be of any use to anybody. I was not a rebellious teenager (after all, you couldn't get in too much trouble in Enterprise, Utah, population 350) but I was very curious and active and asked my parents a lot of questions. I suppose I just had all of the fears and frustrations of an average teenager. I especially remember thinking that maybe my life would be lived more with a whimper than a bang, to paraphrase T. S. Eliot.

It was at that age that I read for the first time in my life

Romans, chapter 8, verse 28: "And we know that all things work together for good to them that love God." I was struck dumb for a minute. Speechless! I remember that moment as if it were locked in time. I was sitting on my white Martha Washington bedspread surrounded by sea blue walls, my head resting on a red velvet pillow. I remember gripping the scriptures as I sort of looked up and said, "Heavenly Father, do you mean that everything that I have ever done, silly or not, good or bad, happy or sad, will come together for my good if I—just love you?" I was incredulous. I can't tell you the joy that filled my heart.

At fifteen I hadn't had too many such moments with what really was pure and beautiful revelation. The whole thing was wonderful. I already knew that I loved God; I just didn't know how deeply until that moment. And at that very instant, I knew that God loved me. I didn't know everything I needed to be forgiven of but I felt—forgiven. I think there on that Martha Washington bedspread with a red pillow, I knew for the first time that I could and would truly be helped in my life and if it was a whimper instead of a bang—well, that would be my fault and certainly not God's. If I could document the moments when I moved from a youthful view of God to a more mature one, to some beginning of what it meant to love him with a maturing heart and mind, one of those moments was that day with Romans 8:28.

Forgive me for that very personal and homey little story. But it is an important moment in my life, and it convinced me that I could rise above sorrows or disappointments or mistakes or despair. I felt that day that God was like an artist. He would use the very stone of my plain, even pitiful little life and refashion it, producing something far more redeeming and substantial. I knew even in that short span of life in Enterprise, Utah, that I might have to endure sometimes painful sculpting, indeed as with a hammer or chisel, if I were to become something precious from this stone. In a softer image I believe we need to be as malleable as clay, and from time to time feel the loving touch of his hand, if we wish him to form more exquisite lines and tones. At that moment I trusted God perfectly, as perhaps only a fifteen-year-old can trust him.

I know it is easier to have that kind of faith in your youth, long before you have suffered through some of life's later challenges, the desperations of the mind that can come. But I think it is sometimes too easy for us to dismiss the faith of youth. That is a cop-out on our part, as the kids would say. Surely these youthful experiences in forming a testimony, which we have all had, must be among those reasons that Christ said, "Become as a little child" (3 Nephi

11:38). I ask us to be like a child, to love God and trust God and keep our eye single to his glory—especially in times of stress and difficulty. I do know that all things will work together for our good. I promise you that on good authority. I promise it on the authority of God's own word.

Some of you may be asking, "How do we do this; how do we make the transition from moments of strength and powerful testimony and spirituality to that world of woe that confronts us from time to time?" My answer is not new, and it has everything to do with covenants—the promise that if we will remember something as fundamental as our baptismal, sacramental, and temple covenants, we will carry an inner peace that God is with us. Knowing precisely the doubts and difficult moments all of us would face, the great Jehovah said to the children of Israel, *"For I know the things that come into your mind, every one of them. . . . yet will I be to [you] as a little sanctuary. . . . I will put a new spirit within you"* (Ezekiel 11:5, 16, 19; emphasis added).

Having gone into the waters of baptism, or to sacrament meeting, or to the temple to make our covenants, we cannot—as much as we would like to—always remain in those wonderfully safe settings. We know that. We have to shoulder our packs and take up the journey again. But that wonderful promise from the Lord just quoted from the book of Ezekiel is that if we cannot always *be in* God's sanctuary, we can always have God's sanctuary *be in us*. "I will be your sanctuary," he promises. "I will put a new spirit within you." When difficult times come, when we realize things are not good the way they are, we trust in God, who can provide a new spirit. That is the power of covenant making and covenant keeping.

So often we hear discussions about our covenants with God, and well we should. Those promises and convictions, this way of faithful living, as someone recently said, "is our ticket home." But sometimes those covenants seem almost too challenging for our inadequate selves to accomplish.

What we too often fail to realize is that at the same time we covenant with God, *he is covenanting with us*—promising blessings, privileges, and pleasures our eyes have not yet seen and our ears have not yet heard. Though we may see *our* part in the matter of faithfulness going by fits and starts, by bumps and bursts here and there, *God's* part is sure and steady and supreme. We may stumble but he never does. We may falter but he never will. We may feel out of control but he never is. The reason the keeping of covenants is so important to us is at least partly because it makes the contract so binding to God. Covenants forge a link between our telestial, mortal struggles and God's celestial, immortal powers.

We bring all we can to the agreement, even if that

doesn't seem like much—our heart, our devotion, our integrity—we bring as much as we can, but he brings eternity to it. He brings himself, priesthood and principalities, power and majesty beyond our wildest imagination. Just listen to the sure language of God's covenantal promise to us: "For the mountains shall depart and the hills be removed, but my kindness shall not depart from thee, neither shall the covenant of my peace be removed, saith the Lord that hath mercy on thee" (3 Nephi 22:10).

God is saying in effect, "Think of the most unlikely things in the world, things like the mountains departing and the hills being removed—think of the most preposterous events you can imagine, but still even then 'my kindness shall not depart from thee, neither shall the covenant of my peace be removed.'" He goes on then and gives the Nephites lovely promises of temporal blessings and this promise from verse 13: "And all thy children shall be taught of the Lord; and great shall be the peace of thy children." I simply cannot imagine a more powerful or hopeful promise.

The danger, of course, is that in times of pain or sorrow, times when the obedience and the sacrifice seem too great (or at least too immediate), we hesitate, we pull back from this divine relationship. How often when we have been asked to give our hearts, or give something from our hearts, or give that latter-day sacrifice of "a broken heart and a contrite spirit"—how often when there is a difficult time or a bruising of our soul, we shy away or openly retreat from a total and uncompromised trust in the one person who knows exactly how to accept our gift and return it tenfold. God knows how to receive a broken heart, bless it, and give it back healed and renewed. He knows how to weep with love over such an offered gift, immediately bless it, mend it, and return it.

With God, whatever has become broken can be fixed. God doesn't just pull out the tiny spikes that life's tribulations have driven into us. He doesn't simply pull out what one writer has called "the nails of our own guilt," leaving us bleeding and scarred forever. No, when we can finally trust our lives, our hearts, our whole souls to the Great Physician, he not only heals what *was* but goes one better and makes all things new. We must remember, as my doctor son-in-law, Lee McCann, would say, "We are up against a surgeon here whose only determination is to heal us—and he knows *exactly* how to do that!" He gives us a new strength of soul, a new birth, a new heart, holier and happier, healthier than it ever was before.

I know that just saying all of this doesn't necessarily make it easy to do. We sing that sacrifice brings forth the blessings of heaven but we know from experience that sacrifice is not a trivial thing, that it can bring sorrow with a

very personal price tag attached. We can sometimes be terrified at what may be asked of us. It reminds me of Sister Hinckley's response when someone asked her how she felt about being the wife of the newly ordained prophet. Stretching to her full four feet, eight inches of height, and with her big brown eyes opened wide, she said, "Oh, I just want my mama!"

I think Sister Hinckley and I would agree with the sentiment expressed by the Apostle Paul, "It is a fearful thing to fall into the hands of the living God" (Hebrews 10:31). "What," we say, "you mean that Paul, who seemed the very essence of courage and faith, talked about being fearful, and fearful over falling into the hands of God at that?" Yes, that very same Paul. And those "afflictions" as he calls them, come "after ye were illuminated," after those moments of having received light, knowledge, power, and revelation. We make our covenant, we step forward with our offering, and then we stand absolutely speechless, even a little terrified, sometimes sobbing with consternation when that offering is accepted.

I am quick to say honestly that I have experienced this pattern in my life, enough times that I am embarrassed to try to count them. The embarrassing part is that I can get lost in the self-preoccupation and self-pity that can come with a little fright and anxiety. I forget too easily what price we must pay for God's precious gift of faith. I forget how many times God will ask us to practice our virtues, embrace our fears, and reiterate our covenants until they are truly established, strengthened, and settled in our souls forever (see 1 Peter 5:10). What we all sadly forget in the heat of battle is that after these tests and tribulations, when God really is satisfied that we are "settled" firmly in the faith, then come the blessings that are too glorious for mere words. I stand as a witness that my most precious blessings, miracles, and the realization of God's covenantal promises have come after my fears have been aroused, my faith has been tried, and my heart truly broken in humility and supplication.

Paul, knowing these fears and frustrations, these fluctuating feelings, pleads with us, "Cast not away therefore your confidence, which hath great recompense of reward. For ye have need of patience, that, after ye have done the will of God, ye might receive the promise" (Hebrews 10:35–36). What then follows in this scriptural sequence is one of the greatest chapters on faith in all the Holy Bible. For the forty verses of the eleventh chapter of Hebrews, Paul describes the faith that preceded the sacrifices and afflictions of Abel, Enoch, Noah, Abraham, Isaac, Jacob, Sarah, Joseph, Moses, Samson, David, and Samuel—to name a few. He recounts there the examples of women who saw their dead raised to life again, accounts of the quenching of fire, escaping the edge of the sword, stopping the mouths of lions, and a host of weaknesses being made strong.

When I think of this kind of faith in the face of adversity and understandable fear, I think of a very current example. Shortly after Elder Neal A. Maxwell's leukemia was detected and he underwent his first chemotherapy treatments, my husband and I went to the hospital to visit with him. He was so sick and fragile and frail. I'll never forget the sweet look on his face and the tear-filled eyes as he softly spoke and said, "I just hope that I do not shrink from this cup which has been given me."

That was several years ago, and he is still serving without shrinking—walking by faith, knowing that he still has leukemia, and never knowing for sure what the Lord may have in store for the next leg of the race. The treatments go on, the nausea returns, the hair comes and goes, but there is Neal Maxwell with his shoulder to the wheel. Elder Maxwell and his wife, Colleen, are perfect modern examples of faith overcoming fear, of hope tinged with sadness, of light shining in otherwise dark moments, of a couple who will never shrink nor shun the fight. To be around them is to feel an aura of serenity and calm. You know that Christ has pleasure in the strength of their covenants.

In these current times, many people are starting to worry

over the calamities of the last days. Fear is waxing strong, and the hearts of some men and women grow cold. To that I say as they do in Australia, "No worries, mate!" Curl up comfortably in your favorite easy chair, wrap yourself in the loving spirit of God, and read the italicized heading for Third Nephi, chapter 22: "In the last days, Zion and her stakes shall be established, and Israel shall be gathered in mercy and tenderness—They shall triumph."

Let me close as I began—with the winds of adversity, shafts in the whirlwinds from the adversary himself. Recently we experienced the worst windstorm Bountiful has seen in several decades. The wind on the freeway was gauged at 113 miles an hour. Coming out of our canyon, it seemed even more than that. Just as I was hearing news reports of semi trucks—twenty of them—being blown over on the roadside, I looked out my lovely back window down toward our creek and saw one of our large trees go down with a crash. Another smaller one followed almost immediately.

For a moment, I confess, I was truly fearful. It was very early in the morning, and Jeff was just leaving for the office. I said to him, "Do you think this is the end? Is it all over—or about to be?" My husband, who has deep faith and endless optimism, took me in his arms and said, "No, but wouldn't it be wonderful if it were? Wouldn't it be wonderful if Christ really did come and his children really were ready for him? Wouldn't it be terrific if evil was finally conquered, once and for all, and the Savior of the world came down in the midst of the New Jerusalem to wipe away *every* tear from *every* eye? Yes," my husband said, "in lots of ways I wish it were the end, but it's not. It is just a stiff windstorm in Bountiful. We have got more work to do." So he kissed me and drove off to work, with trees falling and rafters rattling. (His kisses have that kind of effect on me!)

Now, I was *probably* imagining it, but I *thought* I could hear him whistling a few bars of "Master, the Tempest Is Raging," especially that lovely closing refrain, "Peace, be still; Peace, be still" (*Hymns*, no. 105).

"They mount up to the heaven, they go down again to the depths; their soul is melted because of trouble. They reel to and fro, and stagger like a drunken man, and are at their wits' end. *Then they cry unto the Lord in their trouble,* and he bringeth them out of their distresses. He maketh the storm a calm, so that the waves thereof are still. Then are they glad because they be quiet; so he bringeth them unto their desired haven" (Psalm 107:26–30; emphasis added).

This is God's covenant of peace to you. His kindness shall not depart from you, and terror shall not come near you. God's covenant of peace shall not be removed, for he has so declared.

Index

About the Author

Patricia T. Holland has served as a member of the Young Women general presidency of The Church of Jesus Christ of Latter-day Saints. A popular speaker and writer, she has had several talk tapes published and is the co-author of *On Earth As It Is in Heaven*. She and her husband, Elder Jeffrey R. Holland of the Quorum of the Twelve Apostles, are the parents of three children. They live in Salt Lake City, Utah.